Guiding the Development of Foreign Students

K. Richard Pyle, *Editor*
University of Texas, Austin

NEW DIRECTIONS FOR STUDENT SERVICES
MARGARET J. BARR, *Editor-in-Chief*
Texas Christian University

M. LEE UPCRAFT, *Associate Editor*
Pennsylvania State University

Number 36, Winter 1986

Paperback sourcebooks in
The Jossey-Bass Higher Education Series

Jossey-Bass Inc., Publishers
San Francisco • London

#1aat 7475
(80# 63310)

K Richard Pyle (ed.).
Guiding the Development of Foreign Students.
New Directions for Student Services, no. 36.
San Francisco: Jossey-Bass, 1986.

New Directions for Student Services
Margaret J. Barr, *Editor-in-Chief;* M. Lee Upcraft, *Associate Editor*

New Directions for Student Services (publication number USPS
494-090) is published quarterly by Jossey-Bass Inc., Publishers.
Second-class postage paid at San Francisco, California, and at
additional mailing offices. POSTMASTER: Send address changes to
Jossey-Bass Inc., Publishers, 433 California Street, San Francisco,
California 94104.

Editorial correspondence should be sent to the Editor-in-Chief,
Margaret J. Barr, Sadler Hall, Texas Christian University,
Fort Worth, Texas 76129.

Library of Congress Catalog Card Number LC 85-644751

International Standard Serial Number ISSN 0164-7970

International Standard Book Number ISBN 1-55542-993-9

Cover art by WILLI BAUM

Manufactured in the United States of America

Ordering Information

The paperback sourcebooks listed below are published quarterly and can be ordered either by subscription or single copy.

Subscriptions cost $40.00 per year for institutions, agencies, and libraries. Individuals can subscribe at the special rate of $30.00 per year *if payment is by personal check.* (Note that the full rate of $40.00 applies if payment is by institutional check, even if the subscription is designated for an individual.) Standing orders are accepted.

Single copies are available at $9.95 when payment accompanies order. (California, New Jersey, New York, and Washington, D.C., residents please include appropriate sales tax.) For billed orders, cost per copy is $9.95 plus postage and handling.

Substantial discounts are offered to organizations and individuals wishing to purchase bulk quantities of Jossey-Bass sourcebooks. Please inquire.

Please note that these prices are for the academic year 1986–1987 and are subject to change without notice. Also, some titles may be out of print and therefore not available for sale.

To ensure correct and prompt delivery, all orders must give either the *name of an individual* or an *official purchase order number.* Please submit your order as follows:

Subscriptions: specify series and year subscription is to begin.
Single Copies: specify sourcebook code (such as, SS1) and first two words of title.

Mail orders for United States and Possessions, Latin America, Canada, Japan, Australia, and New Zealand to:
Jossey-Bass Inc., Publishers
433 California Street
San Francisco, California 94104

Mail orders for all other parts of the world to:
Jossey-Bass Limited
28 Banner Street
London EC1Y 8QE

New Directions for Student Services
Margaret J. Barr, *Editor-in-Chief;* M. Lee Upcraft, *Associate Editor*

Contents

Editor's Notes

Student affairs professionals have an opportunity to make a valuable contribution to international understanding and human development. This contribution can be made through a dynamic and ever-increasing resource—the foreign student. However, to take full advantage of this resource it is important that we become knowledgeable about foreign students' unique needs and the approaches and methods appropriate for recruiting and assimilating them into campus culture. Who are these students? What ethical considerations affect their recruitment and their involvement on campus? What approaches should we be aware of in advising and counseling them? How can we best prepare for their increasing numbers? These are a few of the questions examined in this volume.

Currently, the international dimension of student affairs is not at the forefront of the student development movement. National meetings tend to focus on issues outside the purview of foreign students. Commission X of American College Personnel Association (ACPA), entitled "International Dimensions of Student Development," is one of the association's smaller bodies. The professional work on behalf of foreign students is primarily left to the National Association of Foreign Student Affairs (NAFSA) and the International Society for Intercultural Education Training and Research (I-SIETAR). These organizations, although doing effective work, are made up primarily of advisers and directors of foreign students. Input and involvement by the many other student affairs professionals who significantly affect the lives of foreign students is lacking. It is often said that foreign students are an isolated part of the campus, with little interaction with the mainstream. The same might also be said regarding the international office and staff who work with foreign students. This sourcebook is designed to help student affairs professionals understand foreign students, and also to stimulate thinking on how to assist foreign students in their development. It is also hoped that student affairs professionals will see the interesting ways in which foreign students can enrich campus life.

What barriers inhibit foreign students' involvement in campus life?

Many people contributed to the preparation of this sourcebook. I especially appreciate the time and effort expended by the authors, and the assistance of Margaret J. Barr, Editor-in-Chief of this series. The members of the directorate of Commission X of ACPA were invaluable resources in shaping the content and areas of emphasis. Finally, my family and parents, who supported my interest and involvement in the Peace Corps during an earlier phase of my career, are to be commended for their support, which has allowed me to fulfill my interest in and love for the international arena—K R. Pyle.

How can student affairs professionals counter these barriers and promote healthy interaction among culturally varied students? Edith and Emil Spees focus on these questions and their answers in Chapter One. They provide a number of interesting scenarios that give insight into ways to internationalize a campus.

In Chapter Two, Jill Bulthuis addresses the question of who foreign students are and outline their demographic makeup as well as some attitudes and concerns of foreign students. This chapter examines the values, expectations, and assumptions that cause difficulties and conflicts for foreign students, including such issues as time, friendships, equality, and pedagogy.

In Chapter Three, Mark Thackaberry and Antoinette Liston discuss the recruitment and admission of foreign students and provide an overview of the factors and pressures surrounding these processes. They pay special attention to matters of ethics that need to be attended to as pressure grows on admissions offices to recruit foreign students. The authors provide guidelines to assist admissions offices and student affairs divisions to establish policies in this area.

The critical question of how foreign students can be integrated into the campus community and life on campus is discussed in Chapter Four by Margaret Kidd and Richard Reiff. These foreign student professionals share the knowledge and expertise they have acquired over several years of working with foreign students. They suggest a variety of approaches and programs that can assist the adaptation and adjustment process and that may enhance the campus community.

In Chapter Five, Ron Cadieux and Bea Wehrly describe the crucial area of advising and counseling foreign students and examine the unique needs of the sojourner in a foreign country that must be addressed in the advising and counseling process. Particular emphasis is placed on the phases of adaptation, the powerful impact of culture on behavior, and the need to empathize with the value systems of international students.

In Chapter Six, Paul Marion discusses the existing literature about foreign students. Marion reports on a host of research studies focusing on admissions and academic performance, comparisons of nationalities, interaction between American and foreign students, the psychological and social impact of studying abroad, and the relationship of academic achievement to attitudes and adjustment. A bibliography is provided at the end of the chapter.

Chapter Seven, by Barbara Clark and Richard Pyle, provides a thought-provoking scenario for the future. Trends, issues, and implications for higher education are highlighted. Clark makes a number of important recommendations and outlines the challenges that must be met to assist foreign students' development while internationalizing the college campus.

K Richard Pyle
Editor

K Richard Pyle is a counseling psychologist at the University of Texas and has management responsibilities for the campus career development program. He has served as a Peace Corps volunteer and Training Center director and is presently active as a consultant to the Peace Corps. For the past seven years he has directed an international service/learning program for students in Jamaica.

Attitude and an ingenious focusing process permit any size,
type, or location of institution to develop an international
dimension.

Internationalizing
the Campus:
Questions and Concerns

Edith C. Spees, Emil R. Spees

A new student from Taiwan walks into an adviser's office
for the first time to get assistance with course selection. The
adviser quickly goes over the schedule with emphasis on
departmental needs. The student walks away puzzled and
culturally unable to negotiate with this authority figure.

The Iranian Student Association president gets permission to hold a rally in the free speech area of campus
from a student union professional. On the day of the rally
there is an international confrontation in that area when the
equally politically active Iraqi Student Association arrives
prior to the scheduled demonstration and refuses to leave,
arguing that the free speech area cannot be reserved. The
police call the student union director for guidance.

Several residents from family housing call the housing office to complain about violent fights and arguments
taking place in one apartment. When called to the director's

K R. Pyle (ed.). *Guiding the Development of Foreign Students.*
New Directions for Student Services, no. 36. San Francisco: Jossey-Bass, Winter 1986.

office, the African resident and head of household is amazed and offended that anyone would interfere with his conjugal rights, especially within his home.

Why Internationalize?

Since such thorny issues are ever present concerns for academic administrators of international programs, why have an international program? Certainly, to justify such programs the benefits must outweigh the costs.

The problem-solving processes needed for internationalizing campuses are identical to the skills needed to manage our own home towns: Getting food, mediating violent resident altercations, debating conflicting political and moral codes, and administering various departments require intercultural as well as technical skills. We need to understand how human passions work and that they cannot simply be legislated or regulated into safe channels. We need ways to shake up and redefine issues; only then will we gain new insights on basic issues. We even need to highlight the disasters and distresses that can accompany international programs. There is much that can be learned by analyzing a process that went astray.

An active international program is a microcosm of humanity. It is a laboratory for learning how to live and interrelate in a complex world. Developing an international program is the most efficient and realistic way to teach and learn to understand and cope with life's problems in any country or culture. Our nation and the world are cross-cultural communities. The age of homogeneous living groups is past. We must understand this diversity in order to survive.

The average undergraduate college student is no longer eighteen to twenty-two years old, white, middle class, and Protestant. Persons of all races, religions, ages, and economic and cultural backgrounds use the educational system for their own needs and desires. There are intercultural conflicts about language, mores, eating habits, and ways of interfacing with the educational system on every campus. Intercultural marriages, political clashes, approaches to the honor code of agreed-upon rules of academic integrity, and other issues are changing traditional rules and regulations of academic institutions. These intercultural conflicts require a new approach to maintaining international programs on campus.

Coping with Disasters and Distress on Campus

There are many ways international programs can fail. However, logic can reveal why disasters occur. Origins of problems can be traced and, as with other institutional planning, preventive and corrective measures can be taken.

Disasters can result from misunderstandings and from offenses resulting from varying moral and cultural beliefs and from ignorance or thoughtlessness. Prejudices of local and foreign persons, human factors such as loneliness and the need for comfort or security, and vast differences between economic resources and expectations of material goods complicate many relationships and programs. Culture shock is a frequent difficulty.

One Chinese student association at a Midwest university that has a sophisticated international program experienced such distress. Five groups of Chinese students attend that campus: Chinese from Taiwan, Hong Kong, Malaysia, Singapore, and mainland China.

When Taiwanese students wanted to celebrate their National Founding Day, they planned an attraction that would involve American students—food! The Taiwanese students decided to have what Americans call a bake sale of home-cooked Chinese foods to be put on in a popular central location. The students went to the proper officials and obtained written permission, bought and prepared the food, and organized their student group to be ambassadors of goodwill and information about Taiwan.

At the last hour, when most of the students were cooking, an administrator revoked their privilege because the program seemed like a dinner rather than a bake sale. He invoked health department regulations, although his own department regularly bent those guidelines for American functions such as football tailgate parties.

The Chinese students had no recourse; their adviser was unable to communicate the significance of the event to the administrator. The students ate their own food at a private and very ethnic celebration of their Independence Day. The "Ugly American" had struck again.

One sad result of this story is that many years later several of these students will reach high government positions and will tell this story to their colleagues. They will tell how they met the letter and spirit of the regulations and how the bureaucrat did not. They will also tell how he said that they must not have obtained permission and that these doctoral students just did not understand English. Even sadder for the university is the opportunity lost to American students to meet foreign students in such an open and casual way.

At another university the informal policy of the student work-study program has been to put foreign students on midnight janitorial duty so that they would have fewer problems with language barriers. Actually, the policy developed because administrators felt that foreign students would accept these working conditions more readily than would American students. This practice is a discriminatory policy and does nothing to enhance these students' understanding of their own educational processes or of American culture. Since many of these students will be government officials in their own countries within a few years, this ignorant policy is harmful to many interests.

On an individual note, one student who attained only a B average took his own life in the most humiliating form for his culture because he felt he was disgracing his family. Such personal tragedies resulting from cultural expectations are not always preventable, but skilled counselors and advisers can help. They can be alert to warning signs and stay actively involved with various national groups in order to understand the distress that motivates such persons.

Distress also occurs in the multicultural melting pot of American life. The wise administrator must focus on these issues and potential disasters. We see similar behavior between urban and rural students, different religious groups, politically conservative and liberal individuals, the economically advantaged and disadvantaged, and others. When students are from an international rather than national group, only the details of the culture and the expectations change. Human nature does not vary, nor do procedures that can go astray because of individual ignorance, prejudice, or self-serving interests.

The United Nations as a Model. The United Nations (UN) is an example of how these matters can be handled. The UN is a forum for most nations; it is also a community within itself, with its own cultural and legal rules for appropriate behavior. Individuals often transgress the rules, and representatives of different countries are often shocked and offended at the behavior of other members. Educational insititutions must look to the UN for an example of how to address major differences within the philosophical and procedural guidelines it has established in the United Nations Charter.

Full-time mediators at the UN guide individual members through the agonizing process of resolving seemingly insolvable problems. The need for clear communication, deep understanding of personal and national sensitivities, alternative forms of conflict resolution, and respect for the integrity of the individual are essential. People with such skills make the organization viable. The newly developing Peace University model at George Mason University, which offers an M.S. degree in mediation, and other graduate programs in conflict resolution help develop skills in arbitration, community development, family mediation, and psychology to address the theories and techniques of conflict resolution.

The Campus as a Mini United Nations. Any campus with even a few foreign-born faculty, staff, or students automatically qualifies as a mini United Nations. Persons responsible for organizing campus structure tend to impose the dominant culture on this structure. In an international program, it is essential to recognize and address minority differences. To address does not mean to cater to or to manipulate. It means understanding and consistently responding to the international minority in a chosen pattern or focus of interest. How to make this work on a campus without undue disasters and distress is the administrative challenge this chapter addresses.

Making International Programs Work

Attitude. The secret to internationalizing the campus lies in attitude not resources. First, there must be a clear vision of the immediate benefits of an international program to the local population. The need for the program must be compelling. The goals must be clear and logical. The community must be aware that something of interest is taking place. Later, more complex program components can be added.

An *internationalizer* is a person who has this vision and who can gain community support and resources. This person can be a faculty member, an administrator, a community benefactor, or a student. He or she must generate curiosity and create a focused interest in sharing significant community events or experiences. The internationalizer connects local events to the international scene. The idea should not be too unfamiliar at first. It needs to be "sold" as a variation on a familiar theme. Events follow focused planning. Programs follow events. International interest results from a series of successful events.

Support. The internationalizer must develop a network of interested parties, resources, and supporters. This network will work with key administrators or community leaders. Insistent focus on key issues and continuing rewards to responsive persons and programs are essential. Administrators and faculty must be aware that these key people give more than lip service to such activities.

In staff meetings the program leader must make the case for internationalizing the campus and monitor the activities of departments. In a mathematics department, for example, questions regarding the use of international teaching assistants might include: What educational background does a particular country use that makes its graduate students excellent mathematics instructors? Can we generate this excellence here by using these students to teach in this department? What about the language barrier, especially pronunciation and phrasing by foreign lecturers? Is this a barrier to native students in learning mathematics? Can we build a base for excellent student exchanges with another country through regular use of its top students in teaching positions? Are our math professors offering adequate mentoring for these international student instructors? Will these students feel used by the department, or will they be loyal alumni fifteen years from now?

Such discussion must be reported to deans, vice presidents, and the president. How do foreign math instructors fit into the rest of the campus program? What about food and housing? What about financial aid from their country? Is the math department's experience useful to the language program or the engineering program? Does it strengthen the semester abroad program or benefit faculty applications for grants?

Active support of this type costs nothing. It generates connections. It stimulates people to create new aspects of existing programs. It focuses discussion on the existing organization, and this in itself is a healthy administrative activity. Such discussion also identifies active personnel and available material resources. It provides a continuing internal evaluation of policies.

Problem Identification. *Reframing* is a major problem-solving component used by business and human services for identifying and clarifying issues. It involves focusing on an issue from several perspectives and exploring the relationships of the main issue with secondary issues from a variety of positions. In teaching mathematics, for example, the foreign teaching assistant's perspectives may be focused on covering technical details to show the sophistication of mathematics. Students may hope for a simplified outline because they are apprehensive about math. The math department chairperson may be intent on preparing math majors for the sequence of courses locally available. The president of the institution may hope the math program will enhance the research status of the campus.

In this math department example, faculty members may present departmental goals and operational objectives to the dean. The dean may compare these goals with those of other departments and encourage discussion among departmental executive officers. Graduate and undergraduate student evaluations of projected programs should be considered. The overall goals of the institution and the operational realities of resources can be added at the vice presidential level. Faculty and administration can be coordinated at this level so that educational policy, fiscal management, and institutional assets can provide a single thrust to the focused objective. Admissions and housing departments as well as faculty and community should know of the planned policies. All these groups must think through issues that may arise. These groups must ask questions, voice objections, and indicate attitudes and procedures that may affect the proposed plan. Reframing continues as activities proceed and is effective in evaluation sessions after activities and for periodic procedural review.

These various ways of framing issues, with concurrent expectations, must be thought out before results can be expected from a program that employs international teaching assistants. Diverse expectations can be mutually compatible or met only if addressed. It will be clear to the internationalizer that various perceptions of reality exist and must be addressed.

Personnel. Although several personality types and training backgrounds are suitable for the role of internationalizer, the rigors of the job might best be met by combining human services and management skills training. International experience should be required. Knowledge of a second language is also important. Above all, good listening skills and respectful curiosity may identify the natural facilitator who can learn the necessary techniques on the job. Being responsible for international students means being prepared to confront basic life issues: survival in the community, education, family problems, problems with diet, visa and work permit problems, mental health crises, adjustment to local customs; and interpretation and reframing of issues so the dominant community becomes educated about the assimilation process.

The National Association for Foreign Student Affairs (NAFSA) is a gold mine of resources on the complexities of international programming and of international government regulations. NAFSA's members include full- and part-time foreign-student advisers, vice presidents of international relations, and administrative personnel responsible for day-to-day office operations. Members may be student personnel educators, academics, researchers, or community members who are interested in or have a specialty in an international area. The diversification in membership results in a holistic approach to the concerns that this chapter addresses.

Other professional groups that are concerned with international issues include the American Association for Counseling and Development (AACD) and its several subdivisions; the International Society for Intercultural Education, Training, and Research (I-SIETAR); the American Association for Higher Education (AAHE); the National Council on Family Relations (NCFR); the American Association for State Colleges and Universities (AASCU); and the Association of College Unions–International (ACU-I). Members of these organizations actively network practical ideas, are up to date in the current research, and produce many excellent publications. Many other academic organizations have international connections and meetings. Other resources are the bulletins and grant listings published by government agencies, universities, and foundations. Useful addresses are listed at the end of this chapter.

Scope. Delimiting goals will help avoid unrealistic promises of service which tend to destroy credibility. Good management requires studying the most basic needs first. Then secondary priorities can be added and can create a philosophic pattern that gives direction to action. Next, activities should be monitored for quality and scope, and, finally, programs should be evaluated so that they fit into the context of institutional goals.

Developing a three-year and ten-year plan will provide a short- and long-range focus for what will eventually be a long-range program. Finding the right internationalizer, pinpointing key people to provide support, reframing issues to clarify priorities, identifying resources that others might not have seen as valuable to the program, and planning a small, well-designed project that can succeed and be visible are all initial strategies. Clarity of purpose enhances public relations. Creative thinking in the planning process attracts competent leaders who would not waste time on prosaic activities. Identifying local points of view and anticipating community reactions contribute to the "damage control" checklist that must be developed to ensure competent management. Such a network becomes a part of the overall network that all educational institutions use to maintain strength and clarity of purpose.

Size, Type, and Location of Programs

International programs have been successful in large and small, public and private, urban and rural academic institutions across the nation. These programs demonstrate strategies for internationalizing campuses by using thoughtful and well-planned programs supported by key people on the campus and in the community.

Campus Programs. One small rural university encouraged a foreign-born professor to explore product marketing for business administration in another country while on a sabbatical teaching project. The professor brought some useful programs back to students on his home campus and later took students abroad to the same area for locally credited courses in business administration. The student exchange program on campus was enriched as a secondary benefit of this departmental exchange.

Another small educational institution has emphasized programs for local elementary and high school classes. Teaching units on international topics drawn from the cultural resources of the local international community were tested, published, and marketed with the help and expertise of local faculty.

Polish and American chemists have participated in a carefully developed exchange program that developed from professional friendships. Agricultural students from several Third World countries regularly seek out a Midwest campus that emphasizes rice farming. Immigrants from many Southeast Asian countries have settled near community colleges and universities, and as a result dramatic changes in the institutional course offerings have helped integrate these new neighbors into the community. A private liberal arts college has had ongoing exchanges of American and British commonwealth students and faculty for more than sixty years. Many institutions have traditional exchange programs and campus abroad programs that meet their needs for focused, cultural heritage studies.

Role of Community Institutions. Churches, labor unions, cultural centers, high schools, and civic and professional facilities can become involved as program ideas expand beyond the campus. Their interests can include language development, textile design, special education, folk art, airplane mechanics, or agriculture. Research and teaching projects can be developed based on local need or the host country's need of a specific expertise. Private citizens or government officials can visit or host a visit from their peers abroad; goods and technical expertise can be exchanged; and exhibits and demonstrations can be arranged.

A good example of institutional and community cooperation occurred at Our Lady of the Lake University of San Antonio. With the permission of the university president, a key staff member lobbied for and won the privilege of hosting the annual conferences of I-SIETAR, which meets in alternate years in North America and on other continents. The southern Texas location was appealing to the group, especially because it has a Spanish-American heritage and ties to Central and South America. Also, the mayor of San Antonio had been politically active in emphasizing the cross-cultural ties of the region.

The conference selected "International Year of Youth" as its theme and combined a teen program with the adult program. Volunteers from the community ensured that events ran smoothly, even without large convention facilities. Program activities were supplemented by tours of the city. The program featured American minorities, and Spanish Americans, American Indians, and Southeast Asians were encouraged to help develop the program. The conference was a great success. The small private university made a significant contribution to its community, both economically and culturally. The work of the key program developer was warmly appreciated by his academic and local community. It was not surprising that a year later during the catastrophic earthquake in Mexico the mayor of San Antonio was among the leaders of person-to-person relief efforts.

The UN is an example of a group that matches local needs and resources with specific community projects. United Nations Education, Scientific, and Cultural Organization (UNESCO) and the World Health Organization (WHO) have projects and publications available around the world as well as an extensive library for scholars. Students and faculty can receive coordinated kits of materials for a variety of education plans. Self-help, exchange, technical assistance, and information programs are available. When preparing to travel or take a group to another country, guides should contact the professionals from these agencies about specific local issues and concerns.

Community-campus United Nations Association/United States of America (UNA/USA) volunteer support groups have speakers, events, and publications and can provide updated information on a myriad of issues. Many communities have a UNESCO Christmas card booth to help raise funds for UNESCO. This is an excellent place to combine making contacts with other internationalizers with reaching out to local citizens. Halloween can be made productive through the UNESCO trick-or-treat program. This is a favorite project for student involvement, because it establishes young adults as mentors to children. An American student, a foreign student, and a group of American children can have great fun with this service project.

Peace Corps, Friends World Service, Fulbright exchange, and sister city civic exchanges are further examples of existing programs that might appeal to a university, college, or community college's internationalizing efforts. Knowledge and contacts from around the world must be shared with local communities to keep them aware of the significance of these organizations' efforts. For instance, at one university the Peace Corps has funded a graduate assistantship in agriculture. The assistantship was awarded to a former Peace Corps volunteer who is now enrolled in a master's program in community development and the program encourages academic expansion of the fieldwork implemented in other parts of the world. Even students not interested in joining the Peace Corps learn valuable methods of farming, solutions to mechanical problems, and technical strategies from programs sponsored by the Peace Corps. When a foreign country needs several technologies, the university department in agriculture and engineering team with education and communications departments to research the parameters that Peace Corps programs must deliver, while providing for their own students' educational needs.

The business community is both an intriguing and frustrating source of support and practical resources for an international program. The internationalizer may understand how the interests of a given business match beautifully with an international project, but that business will need to be convinced of the program's need. A business's size, objectives, and resources do not necessarily relate to such decisions. There may be important ethnic subgroups in the community, but an officer or a board might make decisions unrelated to the community.

Once a plan is developed, asking for help from a wide variety of businesses is essential. The plan needs to be flexible and must provide several modes of support. Businesses can provide support through letters and public relations projects and by offering the time and services of skilled employees, equipment or supplies that are locally available, or even money. Examples of community business sponsorship are: a designated space in a shopping mall for an international exhibit and food sale; a small ethnic fast-food shop that supports a student from its native country who is attending the local college; a bank that helps with the difficulties of transferring monies from certain regions and also has an officer who advises foreign students about financial alternatives; a local grocery store that carries specialty food for the international population and works with home economists to popularize international cuisine with menus, demonstrations, and support of festival dinners; a business that accepts advanced foreign students in trainee positions; a business that has an annual budget for community donations and public relations funds for a variety of international projects not otherwise fundable.

Raising Expectations. The results of internationalizers' efforts help raise the expectations of others, and expectations lead to local accountability. The internationalization of a campus must be a well-planned effort for each particular institution. The question "How does this help our campus?" must be answered specifically. Most people see education as a tool rather than as an end in itself. "How will a festival of Mexico help me?" "Will I like the music, the food?" These are mundane questions but ones that the festival planners must be able to answer at the planning stage of the event even before financial assistance is sought.

In the examples that introduced the chapter, advisers to Taiwanese (and all international) students need to be trained in advisement skills and trained in the institution's international objectives. The student union director must understand the international policies of the university as well as conflict resolution, and he or she should have a list of personal resources for advice about international confrontation. The housing director, with help from skilled mediators, should likewise seek advice on the cultural implications of the conjugal-community dispute. The community implications as well as the cross-cultural issues that arise in such disputes provide a rich opportunity for educating all participants. Thus potential disasters are converted to well-managed experiences that enrich the diversity of campus life through expanded international contacts. The focus of campus policy has not been diverted but rather expanded. The same techniques work with different cultural groups within this country.

In summary, internationalizing is a process based on attitude: Regardless of the size, type, or location of an institution, a personal commitment from an internationalizer and support from influential persons of the college and the community can create international programs that respond to local need and interest.

Further Resources

Organizations

American Association of Community and Junior Colleges (AACJC)
National Center of Higher Education
One Dupont Circle, No. 410
Washington, D.C. 20036
(202) 293-7050

American Association for Counseling and Development (AACD)
5999 Stevenson Avenue
Alexandria, Va. 22304
(703) 823-9800

American College Personnel Association (ACPA)
5999 Stevenson Avenue
Alexandria, Va. 22304
(703) 823-9800

Association of College Unions–International (ACU-I)
400 East 7th Street
Bloomington, Ind. 47405

Association of International Education Administrators (AIEA)
Office of International Education

Southern Illinois University
Carbondale, Ill. 62901
(618) 536-7735

Foreign Student Service Council (FSSC)
1623 Belmont Street N.W.
Washington, D.C. 20009
(202) 232-4979

International Association of Counseling Services (IACS)
Two Skyline Place, Suite 400
5203 Leesburg Pike
Falls Church, Va. 22041
(703) 820-4710

International Institutional Services (IIS)
380 Madison Avenue
New York, N.Y. 10017
(212) 490-8770

International Society for Intercultural Education, Training, and Research
(I-SIETAR)
1414 Twenty-Second Street, N.W., Suite 102
Washington, D.C. 20037
(202) 296-4710

International Student Service (ISS)
225 Park Avenue, South, Suite 730
New York, N.Y. 10007
(212) 460-5800

National Association for Foreign Student Affairs (NAFSA)
1860 19th Street N.W.
Washington, D.C. 20009
(202) 462-4811

National Association of Student Personnel Administrators (NASPA)
160 Rightmere Hall
1060 Carmach Road
Columbus, Oh. 43210
(614) 422-4445

National Association of Women Deans, Administrators, and Counselors
(NAWDAC)
1325 Eighteenth Street, N.W., Suite 210
Washington, D.C. 20036
(202) 659-9330

National Council on the Evaluation of Foreign Education Credentials (CEC)
Gary Hoover
Associate Dean of Admissions
University of the Pacific
Stockton, Calif. 95204

Publications

American Association for Counseling and Development Journal
Association for College Admissions Counselors Journal
Association of College Unions–International Bulletin
Change
The Chronicle of Higher Education
Current Issues in Higher Education
Educational Record
Higher Education Abstracts
International Journal of Intercultural Relations
Journal of College Student Personnel
Journal of Cross-Cultural Psychology
Journal of Higher Education
Journal of the National Association of Student Personnel Administrators
Journal of Social Issues
National Association of Foreign Student Affairs Newsletter
National Association of Foreign Student Affairs Report of Annual Conference
National Association of Women Deans and Counselors Journal

Books

Hood, M. A., and Schieffer, K. J. (eds.). *Professional Integration: A Guide for Students from the Developing World.* Washington, D.C.: National Association for Foreign Student Affairs, 1984.
Lee, M. Y., Abd-Ella, M., and Burks, L. *Needs of Foreign Students from Developing Nations at U.S. Colleges and Universities.* Washington, D.C.: National Association for Foreign Student Affairs, 1981.
Pearson-Chen, R. *Living Language: People Talk.* Singapore: Federal Publications, 1985.
Wang, G., and Dissanayake, W. (eds.). *Continuity and Change in Communication Systems: An Asian Perspective.* Norwood, N.J.: Ablex Publishing Corporation, 1985.

18

Edith C. Spees is a registered marriage and family therapist with a practice in Carbondale, Illinois. She has been an active member of ACPA Commission X, "International Dimensions of Student Development."

Emil R. Spees is an associate professor in the Department of Educational Administration and Higher Education at Southern Illinois University, Carbondale, and is a past chairperson of ACPA Commission X.

A better understanding of foreign students is crucial
are to be effective facilitators of their growth and dei

The Foreign
Student Today:
A Profile

Jill D. Bulthuis

> *After thorough consideration of the case with our bishops,*
> *abbotts, princes, dukes, judges, and other noblemen of our*
> *high court, we decree this benefit of our grace, that everyone*
> *who because of his studies wanders abroad, students and*
> *professors of the most divine and holy laws, shall themselves*
> *as well as their messengers come in security to places where*
> *studies are exercised and live there in peace . . . who of them*
> *would not be pitied as they for the love of sciences long*
> *exiled, deprived themselves, being already poor of riches,*
> *expose their lives to many dangers and sustain corporal*
> *injuries by often very villainous people.*
>
> > *Frederick I, 1158 A.D.,*
> > *178 Privilegium Scholasticum*

As early as the Middle Ages students and professors were going abroad in search of academic opportunities unavailable at home and accepting the challenge of adapting to strange people and customs. The history of foreign students on United States campuses can be traced to the colonial colleges, but beginning with Francisco de Miranda, who studied

K R. Pyle (ed.). *Guiding the Development of Foreign Students.*
New Directions for Student Services, no. 36. San Francisco: Jossey-Bass, Winter 1986.

early as 1784, foreign students came to this country as individual
ners. Although their numbers were significant enough to be
ded in statistics early in this century, they were considered unusual
d exotic due in part perhaps to their English pronounciation or their
distinctive styles of dress (Barber, 1985).

A massive acceleration of the movement of students and scholars
began after World War II, although foreign students did not begin to
appear in significant numbers until the 1950s (Barber, 1985). With this
large influx, which represented a wide cross section of society, certain
problems became apparent in the adjustment of some students concerning
English language skills, and financial support. Their reasons for coming
to the United States persist among today's foreign students, and in many
cases the challenges they face persist as well. Spaulding and Flack (1976)
concluded that the major reasons foreign students come to the United
States are to get an advanced education or training not available at home,
to gain prestige with a degree from a U.S. institution, to take advantage of
available scholarship funds, to escape unsettled political or economic conditions, and to learn about the United States. When a student from Mexico
City who is studying film at New York University decided he wanted to be
a filmmaker, he decided to come to the United States to study. "If I could
have stayed in Mexico, I would have," he said, "but there is only one film
school there, and it is not a good one" (personal communication). So he
enrolled in the program at New York University. A group of Malaysian
students are studying computer science at a midwestern university because
their government has a training contract with that school. Several students
from El Salvador studying at the University of North Carolina at Chapel
Hill have continued on into graduate programs to avoid returning to the
political unrest at home.

Enrollment Trends

Evangelauf (1985) reported in the *Chronicle of Higher Education*
that the number of foreign students attending U.S. colleges and universities has remained relatively steady for the second year in a row. In
1984-1985 the foreign student population was 342,111. According to the
results of the annual foreign student census of the Institute of International
Education (IIE), the typical foreign student was male, attended a public
four-year institution, studied business or a scientific or technical subject,
and paid his bills with personal or family resources. More students came
from Taiwan than from any other country. The enrollment of students
from South and East Asia increased most in the 1984-1985 period, with
China experiencing the greatest growth, followed by Malaysia and Korea.
Seventy percent of the students were male, 46 percent were studying for
bachelor's degrees, and 36 percent were studying for graduate degrees. Of

the sixty-five percent attending public institutions, two-thirds were paying their own education expenses.

The rate of future flow of foreign students into the United States is predicted in a recent IIE research report (Barber, 1985). A relatively small number of countries (fifteen) account for 60 percent of the foreign students in the United States, and this concentration leaves many American institutions vulnerable to the impact of policy changes of a handful of countries that send their students here.

The number of women among foreign students has been increasing steadily. The United States plays an important role in educating foreign students in engineering, the natural sciences, law, and social sciences. Thirty percent of all foreign students in the United States are enrolled in only 1 percent of the institutions, so greater institutional dispersion in the future seems likely, considering the absorption capacity of institutions. A more equal balance between undergraduate and graduate students is also likely to occur in the near future. These trends reflect the condition of educational resources in all parts of the world. In spite of the IIE total enrollment statistics cited above, the firmest of several projections cited here indicates that by 1991 there will be 698,000 foreign students in the United States, almost double the present number. Since East Asia is gaining economic ground and countries of that region place a high premium on education, wealthy countries with large populations will likely be of far greater significance than small and poor countries. If the People's Republic of China becomes seriously interested in sending students here, the implications for higher education will be dramatic owing to the need for additional services.

Chinese Students. Since Chinese students are generally less prepared for study abroad, they will require comprehensive, balanced support services to ensure adequate adjustment to the language, the educational system, and U.S. culture. College admissions staff will need to develop skill in evaluating credentials from Chinese institutions. Since Chinese people are generally unaccustomed to automobile traffic, safety regulations must be a part of their orientation if they are to avoid accidents. Students in China do not have access to foreign currency exchange, and as a result many have arrived in the United States with insufficient funds to pay their school fees and support themselves adequately. Those who are government sponsored receive lower-than-average stipends; thus their living conditions are frequently substandard and groups live together for reasons of economics and convenience. Institutions with large enrollments of Chinese students and scholars report that support service costs are high and that successful integration of these individuals into the campus community is difficult to accomplish.

Fields of Study. The foreign student population in the United States has grown most rapidly in the fields of business, while the fields of humanities, health, agriculture, and education have shown the smallest relative growth. The fields in which American student interest has dropped most dramatically (humanities and education) are also in relatively low demand by foreign students, while the fields in greatest demand by foreign students are also in high demand by American students (Zikopoülos and Barber, 1985).

Needs of Foreign Students. The influx of foreign students into U.S. colleges and universities in recent years has resulted in countless investigations—some local, others national and international in scope—to study the phenomenon of student sojourners and their experiences in this country. These investigations indicate, however, that it is as difficult to generalize about the expectations, needs, attitudes, experiences, and problems of foreign students as it is to generalize about the schools enrolling them.

The term *foreign student* is clearly too broad for fruitful discussion about students from other countries. The term masks important distinctions based on such matters as country of origin, age, sponsorship, field of study, personal goals in studying abroad, and job opportunities at home. A married graduate student from East Asia is likely to have very different priorities and interests from those of an unmarried Latin American undergraduate. Regarding both as foreign students implies that they have more in common than they do.

Three hundred forty-two thousand students come from more than 150 countries and have dramatically different levels of English language proficiency, academic preparation, financial support, and social skills. These students are attending at least 3,000 schools, each with its own academic program and level of commitment to international education, that are located in communities across the United States (Barber, 1985). A Malaysian graduate student studying engineering at the University of Evansville, Indiana, would describe his or her experiences very differently from an undergraduate German student studying American folklore at the University of Virginia. The financial strain on a student at the University of Southern California is somewhat different from that of a student in a cooperative work-study program at Northeastern University in Boston. Language is a problem for some but not for others. The same disparity is found in the areas of finances, academics, and social life.

Concerns of Foreign Students

Perhaps the most consistent generalizations about foreign students in the United States are those of Iowa State University sociologist, Motoko Lee (1981), who surveyed two thousand foreign students about their most important and best-satisfied needs. Lee developed a profile of the student most likely to have a satisfying educational experience in the United States: a Latin American or European graduate assistant who has good English skills, an American roommate, and a job waiting at home. In general, Lee found that foreign students place much greater importance on their academic and professional goals than they do on nonacademic concerns. Although students were generally satisfied with their progress toward academic goals, their lack of practical work experience and uncertainty about careers were matters of great concern.

Personal experience lends support to Lee's findings. Even students who have suffered serious problems with housing, for example, or with the banking system, the Internal Revenue Service, or with the Immigration and Naturalization Service are inclined to rate academic and financial problems as the most difficult. Foreign student loan funds on many U.S. campuses have kept numerous foreign students afloat while they were waiting for stipends delayed by international conflicts that frequently affect currency transfer controls abroad or when personal or family emergencies have placed unusual demands on their finances.

Given foreign students' diversity of personal experience, cultural distinctions, language experience, and motivations for study in the United States, how can cultural characteristics, attitudes, and patterns about a group as heterogeneous as this be addressed? I will compare and contrast those American values, expectations, and assumptions that cause difficulties and conflicts for students from abroad. (An apology is in order to Canadian and Latin American readers for using the term *American:* I realize that it is an inaccurate and not necessarily inclusive usage.)

Concept of Time. Students from African, Asian, and Latin American countries agree that the pace of life in the United States is fast. Americans are very much on the go, racing from morning to night, frequently taking half an hour to eat lunch while standing up at a counter. Americans are very dependent on the clock, which provides structure in their lives. Movies or other events begin precisely at 7:15 or 9:30, and students rush to make a class that begins at 9:15. New foreign students are amazed when they receive the invitation to the college president's reception in their honor and the invitation reads 7:30–9:30. Whoever heard of telling honored guests when to leave a party? Americans see time as a limited resource, not to be wasted. More university personnel need to realize that there is a different way of viewing the world, a perspective in which time tends to be measured more in days, weeks, and months than in minutes and hours. When invited to a dinner given by West African students, it is a good idea to ask whether it is 7:00 American time or African time, which could mean much later. There is a perspective in other parts of the world that allows for more than a quick "hi" when running into a friend on the street. A Kenyan student points out that in his country there would be more of an exchange of pleasantries when meeting an acquaintance by chance.

Friendships. In this highly mobile society, Americans move an average of fourteen times. When combined with the highly individualistic character for which Americans are well known, the result is a concept of friendship that is less permanent and lasting than friendships in another culture. Americans are described by foreign students at the University of North Carolina as very friendly and approachable but as not following through on their offers. Phrases such as, "Come on over some time," "Let's get together real soon for lunch," "I'll call you," and "Y'all come again real soon," when not followed by a definite invitation, are intended to be meaningless pleasantries. But to many newly arrived foreign students, these exchanges are interpreted as positive signals of sincere interest and friendship.

A five-year study entitled "The Cross-Cultural Student—Lessons in Human Nature" (the "Stick to Your Own Kind" study, as it later became known) conducted at the University of Wisconsin indicated that international students associate most with fellow nationals. These students' warm, intimate, dependent, personally satisfying contacts are almost exclusively limited to their own national group. Their relations with Americans rarely go beyond superficial pleasantries, since they are discouraged about any prospect for deep cross-cultural friendships (Miller, 1971, p. 128).

It appears that despite shared projects, shared picnics, or occasionally shared rooms, the majority of interpersonal contacts fall far short of friendship for these students. Even with the increasing emphasis on internalization and with pressures within the United States for breaking down barriers between different peoples, there is only slight evidence of progress within what should be the most enlightened and tolerant segment of society—the university community.

The result is that foreign students who experience enough interpersonal disappointment or rejection will generally become convinced that the advice to "stick to your own kind," is good.

Foreign student advisers tell the story of Kwame Nkhrumah to demonstrate this isolation. Half a century ago, a poor student from West Africa traveled to this country to attend a university in Philadelphia—a sojourn he would later recall as "years of sorrow and loneliness." He experienced poverty and racism that he had not known in Africa, and he nearly died of exhaustion from working nights and attending class during the day. It was an experience he remembered vividly and often recounted years later after rising to international prominence as the founding father and president of the African nation of Ghana (Herbert, 1981).

Equality. It is not always easy for elite members of hierarchical societies who become graduate students in the United States to see the benefits of an egalitarian system. Accustomed to instantaneous, cordial service at home, they are suddenly faced with making do in the kitchen, grocery store, and laundromat—different territory for many male, and female, students from abroad. To add to the misery, they frequently confront indifferent service people with "I'm as good as you are" attitudes.

These experiences, coupled with a reduced standard of living necessitated by small wages or stipends, can result in what sometimes is called status shock. These students may need help in adapting to the American lifestyle, where working women are also housewives and mothers—and without servants.

For some students this egalitarianism may be most noticeable in the classroom. Foreign students are quick to notice the different student-faculty relationships that exist. It is difficult for many of them to adjust to an open classroom environment in which students can criticize a professor's point of view, informal presentations of opinions are part of the grade, and professors remain involved in serious discussions with students after class or occasionally invite students into their homes. This is unusual for many students who are accustomed to speaking in class only when called on and who have had no contact with faculty members outside the classroom.

Pedagogy. Many societies stress memorization in their education systems, and knowledge is conceived of as a body of facts that students memorize. If students acquire this knowledge or a portion of it, they are considered educated. Americans conceive of knowledge, however, as a constant discovery involving an ongoing search, a creative process requiring a different style of pedagogy.

Many foreign students, students from the Middle East, for example, will initially have difficulties studying in our system. They often have not been trained to do independent library research or to write imaginative or even logical essays. Generally they have only experienced the lecture method of teaching and have been required to memorize facts in preparation for exams once or twice a year. Many of these students are unaccustomed to the constant pressure of pop quizzes, frequent exams, classroom assignments, and term papers and may need some coaching to learn how to adapt.

In an educational system such as ours in which professors often leave the classroom during exams and students do not complete study projects cooperatively unless specifically assigned to do so, students new to the honor code system have been accused of cheating and plagiarism. Cheating by foreign students may be partly explained by the pressure to obtain good grades in order to achieve status and prestigious jobs. This pressure, together with culturally reinforced reliance on personal ties, such as those among fellow students, may result in a higher incidence of plagiarism among certain groups of foreign students. Another explanation may lie in not understanding what plagiarism is. If students have never had to write an essay or term paper and if memorization and factual content have been stressed in their educational experience, they may assume that writing a paper means copying material from a published text. One way to reduce such incidents is to ensure that the definitions of plagiarism and cheating are clearly understood in each educational setting, while keeping in mind that these definitions may be different for a computer science course, a physics laboratory, and a business management class.

Adjustment. In discussing the adjustment problems of foreign students, Howard Smith (1955) emphasized four stages that most students pass through while studying abroad: the spectator stage, the adaptive stage, the coming-to-terms stage, and the predeparture stage.

In the spectator stage, foreign students studying in the United States may suffer nervous fatigue, but the excitement of the experience and the adventure is pleasing. Students are somewhat detached in this stage, and their beliefs and values are not threatened. This first stage ends when students are called to participate in activities or endeavors that are rooted in the American culture and that contradict their values and beliefs. The second, or adaptive, stage is one of unresolved conflict and culture shock in which individual defenses are rallied to counteract numerous stresses. Coming to terms with a new environment marks the third stage, during which students recognize and reassess their own traditional habits, beliefs, behaviors, and attitudes. Students in this stage reject and criticize American culture more freely and choose the kinds and degrees of conformity that will allow them to adapt to American people and customs. They may become more aggressive, diligent, relaxed, or tolerant, but at least they have reached a state of equilibrium. In the predeparture stage, students put American culture into another perspective as they begin to focus on reestablishing themselves in their home countries.

An awareness of the stages in the adjustment process and of the characteristics of American culture that can hinder the adjustment of students from abroad will be useful to counselors, faculty, and student support services personnel who work with foreign students. It will also be helpful for students to understand how the cultural adjustment process can affect their physical and mental health and how to find and use the support systems available to them.

Conclusion

Many traditional student development theories may not apply to foreign students whose value systems differ dramatically from those of Americans. Americans value independence, self-reliance, autonomy, efficiency, time management, and entrepreneurship. Our theories of student development tend to promote such values, character traits, and life patterns. Many foreign students at U.S. colleges and universities arrive with different values and principles. Many come from countries where such things as young single women living alone or independent of their parents, or competition resulting in someone's failure, is virtually unknown. In their culture paying someone money may be the only way to accomplish something, and definitions of male and female roles are clear and rigid. For some, adapting to an American campus is merely a formidable challenge. To others it presents a serious obstacle to accomplishing educational goals. Sensitivity to different cultural expectations concerning classroom behavior, appropriate roles of faculty and staff, and the way services should be provided may alleviate misunderstanding and frustration for all involved.

The foreign students currently in the United States are from many different countries and of various ages. They represent various socioeconomic levels and study every subject available. This diversity makes a profile of the foreign students today difficult to assess. This population has been likened, however, to a good vegetable soup in which the individual vegetables remain whole and identifiable in appearance and taste, yet blend together to create a flavor that is distinct and enriches what otherwise might be bland and homogeneous.

References

Barber, E. G. (ed.). *Foreign Student Flows.* New York: Institute of International Education, 1985.

Evangelauf, J. "Number of Foreign Students in U.S. Rises Less than 1 Percent." *Chronicle of Higher Education,* October 9, 1985, p. 31.

Herbert, W. "Abroad in the U.S.: Foreign Students on American Campuses." *Educational Record,* Summer 1981, pp. 68–71.

Lee, M. Y. *Needs of Foreign Students from Developing Nations at U.S. Colleges and Universities.* Washington, D.C.: National Association for Foreign Student Affairs, 1981.

Miller, M. H. "The Cross-Cultural Student—Lessons in Human Nature." *Bulletin of the Menninger Clinic,* 1971, *34* (2), 128.

Smith, H. P. "Do Intercultural Experiences Affect Attitudes?" *Journal of Abnormal and Social Psychology,* 1955, *51,* 469–477.

Spaulding, S., and Flack, M. *The World's Students in the United States.* New York: Praeger, 1976.

Zikopoülos, M., and Barber, E. G. (eds.). *Profiles, 1983/1984.* New York: Institute of International Education, 1985.

Jill D. Bulthuis is director of the International Center at the University of North Carolina in Chapel Hill. She has been an active member of NAFSA and has recently served as the NAFSA liaison to ACPA Commission X, "International Dimensions of Student Development."

There are a number of significant steps and guidelines to follow if we are to do justice to a quality recruitment and admissions program.

Recruitment and Admissions: Special Issues and Ethical Considerations

Mark D. Thackaberry, Antoinette Liston

Dae Chun Park completed his secondary education in Korea with mediocre results. He then sought admission to a bachelor's engineering program in the United States. After being rejected by several universities, he engaged the services of a professional placement agency located in Korea. For a fee of $1,100 the agency secured Park's admission to an intensive English language program connected with a university that had a highly respected engineering school. Park was verbally assured that the successful completion of the English program constituted admission to the university's engineering program. After six months of study in the United States, Park was disappointed to find that his newly acquired English proficiency would not compensate for his poor academic record. He was again denied admittance to engineering schools and returned to Korea feeling discouraged and disgraced.

Muslinah Binte Abdul Rahman, a Malaysian scholarship student, applied for undergraduate admission to a small northwestern college in the United States. At the end of June she received her acceptance documents. Unfortunately, the immigration form I-20 was incorrectly prepared and the American embassy would not grant her a student visa. By the time

K R. Pyle (ed.). *Guiding the Development of Foreign Students.*
New Directions for Student Services, no. 36. San Francisco: Jossey-Bass, Winter 1986.

Muslinah received a corrected I-20 and visa, the fall classes were already in session, which necessitated a delay until the following semester.

In January Muslinah disembarked from the plane wearing a traditional Malay batik dress and cotton jacket to encounter snow and subzero weather. The college had not included climatic or cultural information in the introductory materials. As she was unfamiliar with the various transportation options, Muslinah secured a taxi for $150 to take her the seventy-five miles to her residence hall. After depositing her luggage in her room, she proceeded to the cafeteria and discovered that the main dish was ham, which was forbidden by her Islamic dietary restrictions. Cold, hungry, and exhausted, she returned to her room in despair.

In the succeeding weeks her disenchantment with the college was accelerated by the refusal of the admissions office to accept her foreign postsecondary study for university credit. Luckily, she was assisted by the Malaysian student department, a Malaysian government agency, in locating another school familiar with the needs of foreign students, and she transferred to it the following semester.

Both Dae Chun and Muslinah were victims of inappropriate foreign admissions practices. These are just two situations that point to the need for sensitive treatment of foreign students. What follows is a discussion of the issues and general guidelines for recruiting and admitting foreign students.

Issues in Foreign Student Admissions

Competition is inherent in the American way of life, as is evident in institutions of higher education and in business. Unlike many countries, there are thousands of institutions in the United States that offer similar degrees, causing colleges to vie for the best, and sometimes the most, students. Methods of recruitment at American institutions follow long-established tradition of competitiveness (Brohm, 1980).

Recruitment of foreign students, however, has historically been perceived differently. Many admissions recruiters have been reluctant to recruit from abroad, and those who do pursue foreign students walk an ethical tightrope. In the latter 1970s several schools fell off this tightrope when ABC television produced an exposé featuring some questionable foreign recruitment practices that included situations similar to Dae Chun's and Muslinah's. The bad press had the positive side effect of spurring professional educators to review their foreign recruitment procedures. Since 1980, the National Liaison Committee on Foreign Student Admissions has provided guidance for professionals regarding international admissions, immigration, and related ethical issues (National Liaison . . . , 1980a).

The availability of such assistance, combined with dire projections of declining domestic enrollments has generated a better image of foreign recruitment throughout academia. Traditional reluctance to recruit from abroad is fading as adherence to ethical standards makes recruitment a viable option. The purpose of this chapter is to present the issues and ethical considerations relevant to foreign admissions and recruitment.

Pre-Recruitment Considerations. Prior to establishing a foreign student recruitment program, the university must be cognizant of the problems inherent in foreign admissions. The institution must assess the relationship of foreign students to the goals of the university. Goodwin and Nacht (1983) recommend that demographic considerations such as the size of the university, quotas, and using foreign students as "fillers" to campus enrollment be addressed.

Demographic Factors. There are a number of opinions about the ideal percentage of foreign students for a university community. If an institution's objective is to enrich American students' international exposure, the desired percentage will often be lower than if the objective is to bolster low enrollment. Unfortunately, there is no magic number, and each situation is unique. For example, Northern Illinois University is a state institution with approximately 25,000 students. The foreign component of the student body numbers almost 1,000, or 4 percent. Although the percentage of foreign students is relatively low, the parochial orientation of the primarily agricultural community (33,000 population) discourages a larger percentage. Institutions such as the University of Southern California (Los Angeles) and Columbia University (New York) enjoy the luxury of urban localities and tolerant atmospheres that can easily accommodate large ethnic minorities.

If an institution finds that its international student population is comprised mainly of students from only a few countries or geographic areas, the institution might consider providing incentives to students from other parts of the world, such as financial aid, specialized programming, or professional opportunities.

The purpose of such an effort is twofold: to provide a more diversified exposure for the campus and to avoid the development of nationality "ghettos"—a large number of students from the same country or region congregated on a single campus. The self-imposed isolation of Malaysian students is currently a common phenomenon throughout the United States (Levitov, 1983).

Institutional Commitment. Any self-assessment by an institution should include its total commitment to international education as well as a consideration of demographic factors. To demonstrate its commitment, the administration should be willing to provide funds for additional admissions personnel, foreign student advisers, and student support systems.

Admissions Personnel. If the program is small, the administration may opt to hire an admissions credentials analyst in lieu of hiring or training additional admissions personnel. However, the admissions authority must remain with the institution. If new staff is hired or existing staff is trained for foreign admissions, the designated personnel must have adequate training in international admissions procedures.

New staff should be aware of the cultural as well as educational needs of students from different countries. Preadmission materials should be sent to all prospective international students to ensure accurate presentation of available programs. This is especially important for universities with intensive English programs. Applicants should be informed that acceptance into an English program may not constitute acceptance into a degree program. Through membership in the American Association of Collegiate Registrars and Admissions Officers (AACRAO), professionals can receive assistance in these areas. Through AACRAO, admissions personnel have access to current information on credential evaluation, criteria for the evaluation of English proficency, and other relevant issues.

Foreign Student Advisers. In addition to admissions personnel, a foreign student adviser familiar with immigration regulations is mandatory. In August 1983 new immigration regulations were enacted that increased institutions' reporting and record-keeping requirements. But immigration expertise alone is not sufficient. The foreign student adviser must also be sensitive to cultural differences and thoroughly knowledgeable of institutional and community resources. These skills are necessary to develop and execute orientation programs, cross-cultural counseling, and general services referrals. Guidance in interpreting immigration requirements and in developing foreign student services is available to foreign student advisers through the National Association for Foreign Student Affairs (NAFSA). The staffing recommendation of NAFSA is one foreign student adviser per 250 internationals.

Support Systems. Institutional commitment should also be reflected in student support systems such as housing and financial aid. Some institutions have found it necessary to lift mandatory residence hall requirements. This accommodates the dietary restrictions of certain ethnic groups and allows institutions to close all dorms for vacation periods. Others, such as Siena Heights College in Michigan, have incorporated provisions for religious and cultural needs in their residency hall food services. The University of Indiana addressed the problem of vacation housing accommodations by keeping one residence hall open for international students during break periods. Community host families or programs such as Christmas International House may meet the vacation housing needs for institutions with a small international population (National Liaison . . . , 1980a).

Financial Support. Foreign students are subject to political changes and fluctuations in international currency rates that necessitate the development of adequate financial support systems. The need for emergency financial support was dramatically illustrated after the 1979 Iranian revolution. An adviser at a Wisconsin university reported that many Iranians were forced to sleep on the flat roofs of dormitories when they were unable to receive money from home, work off campus (because of immigration restrictions), or find alternative financial aid. More recently, Nigerian students have experienced difficulty as Nigerian bureaucratic corruption and the fall in the price of crude oil have rendered cash flow from Nigeria almost nonexistent. Institutions recruiting foreign students must therefore be prepared to provide additional financial resources through short-term loans, on-campus employment, tuition waivers, or other emergency provisions.

Ethical Factors in Foreign Student Admissions. As in all areas of admissions, judgments must be made about the correctness, or ethics, involved in professional recruitment activities. In the United States the availability of education is taken for granted by many, and the choice of institution or academic program is often influenced by modern marketing. Glossy brochures showing ivy-covered buildings and a handsome couple strolling down the college lane have swayed many prospective American students.

However effective these methods may be, they do not provide specific and concrete information for the prospective international student. Specific information concerning courses of study, length of program, cost, relevance to students' career goals in the home country, climate, and living accommodations should be included.

In March 1980 a colloquium was held by the National Liaison Committee (NLC) on foreign student admissions to examine current practices and to establish guidelines on foreign student recruitment. The NLC is composed of the American Association of Collegiate Registrars and Admissions Officers (AACRAO), the College Board, Council of Graduate Schools, Institute of International Education (IIE), and the National Association for Foreign Student Affairs (NAFSA). The colloquium determined nine abuses prevalent in the recruitment of foreign students that are considered detrimental to student welfare and to the reputation of higher education in the United States. The abuses addressed and the guidelines developed by the colloquium provide excellent guidance to institutions wishing to recruit international students in an ethical manner. Owing to their importance, the list of major abuses is included without abbreviation, as follows:

1. The use of placement agencies that charge institutions a per capita fee.

2. The recruitment of foreign students without prior consideration of and commitment to providing necessary campus services.

3. Failure to represent the institution properly in advertising publications, informative materials, personal interivews, and so on.

4. The use of inadequately trained foreign admissions officers.

5. The improper delegation of admissions authority.

6. The misuse of immigration forms with regard to a student's academic qualifications, English language proficiency, and financial resources.

7. The practice of granting admission to English language programs to foreign students who are college bound, without regard to their academic qualifications.

8. The practice of granting foreign students admission to English language programs that do not qualify as full-time intensive programs and are therefore not in compliance with Immigration and Naturalization Service regulations.

9. The practice of promising or implying that admission to intensive English language programs constitutes admission to an academic degree program (National Liaison . . . , 1980a).

Reputable counseling agencies such as American-Midwest Educational and Training Services (AMID-EAST) must charge potential students $150 to $200 in order to process the extensive paperwork. However, disreputable "head hunter" recruitment agencies levy a per capita fee to the school for each student enrolled or charge the applicant $500 to $1,000 for guaranteed placement. The members of the colloquium agreed that the use of these third-party professional recruiters was a highly risky proposition. Unethical methods and misrepresentation can be tempting to the private entrepreneur whose survival depends on placement fees. Subsequent to the March 1980 colloquium, the NLC established a foreign student recruitment information clearinghouse with three main objectives: to gather, organize, and distribute data on private foreign recruitment agencies for educational institutions; to publicize the criteria for ethical recruitment and abuses in foreign recruitment; and to provide guidance to educational institutions in foreign recruitment efforts (National Liaison . . . , 1984).

Whether academic institutions rely on the services of reputable advisement agencies and private credentials analysts, or hire salaried employees for recruitment and admissions, the admissions authority should not be delegated. The school's admissions personnel alone must retain the responsibility for the issuance of the I-20 (the immigration form required to obtain a student visa). It is unethical to give blank, signed I-20 forms to any agent in the field. In addition to reviewing academic credentials, admissions personnel must scrutinize applicants' English proficiency and financial resources prior to the issuance of this document. Trained foreign admissions officers are necessary even in community colleges with open door policies. Such policies must be modified to establish appropriate standards for international students, since the consequences of failure for this population are far higher both financially and emotionally than for Americans.

A common misuse of an immigration form is the granting of an I-20 naming a degree program simultaneous to the issuance of an I-20 for an intensive English program. Applicants will often tell a school that they are unable to obtain a student visa for an English language program without a second I-20 for an academic program. However, it is inappropriate to issue an I-20 for a degree program until the student meets admissions standards. In these situations, the school may issue a letter of acceptance contingent on verification of English proficiency if all other admissions standards are met.

In order to provide guidelines and to avoid abuses, the colloquium cited the following criteria for ethical recruitment:

1. Provide enough candid and pertinent information that a foreign student unfamiliar with United States practices in higher education may make informed academic judgments.

2. Avoid contractual arrangements with agents who require fee-for-enrollment payments.

3. Develop an admissions policy for foreign students that requires that admissions judgments be made by institutional personnel who rule on other admissions, are based on a system of written criteria, and are applied in competition with other applicants.

4. Seek a match between the needs and aspirations of the prospective student and the educational opportunities the institution affords.

5. Accept the commitment to provide effective educational opportunity for foreign students and establish appropriate institutional policies governing foreign student recruitment admissions, support activities, specialized programs, and curricula.

6. Provide realistic estimates of costs for tuition, educational expenses, subsistence, and related fees, and of the extent to which financial aid or scholarships are available to foreign students.

7. Restrict evaluation of foreign academic records to personnel who are trained and competent in interpretation of foreign educational records.

8. State clearly to students admitted to English programs the extent of commitment made for their further education in the United States (National Liaison . . . , 1980a).

Establishing a Foreign Recruitment Program

There are three basic forms of foreign recruitment: active, semiactive, and passive. The word-of-mouth approach, or passive recruitment, flourishes on many campuses. Admissions personnel are accustomed to foreign students and faculty requesting application materials for friends. This method of recruitment is effective only if the academic programs and personal services meet current students' needs.

Employing overseas recruiters and establishing foreign offices constitute the main components of an active recruiting program. The University of Miami deploys admissions staff as recruiters to foreign high schools and counseling centers. The service these recruiters provide includes presenting information about the U.S. educational system, how to select an appropriate institution, costs and financial aid, the application process and testing, and visas and travel (Silney, 1983). In addition to being knowledgeable in the aforementioned areas, representatives must be sensitive to cross-cultural communication and aware of local customs. The itinerary of overseas recruiters must be planned well in advance and should include written confirmation of all planned contacts.

An active program might also include special programs designed for a specific population. For example, Southern Illinois University–Carbondale conducted a nondegree program for Malaysian airforce personnel. The introduction of the new immigration classification of "M" (technical rather than degree-seeking students) is especially well suited for this purpose. Such specialized programs must be carefully developed in institutions experienced in international education.

Schools lacking the funds necessary for such active endeavors might choose to pursue a semiactive recruitment program. This would encompass activities such as annually distributing catalogues to counseling agencies and high schools, developing brochures tailored to international students, fostering foreign alumni groups, and providing financial aid such as tuition waivers or on-campus employment. In addition, faculty with overseas experience are a resource that may be tapped. In this type of recruitment Goodwin and Nacht (1983) found former Peace Corps volunteers, foreign faculty, and American faculty experienced in foreign technical assistance to be enthusiastic advocates of international education.

The identification of appropriate destinations for catalogues and information for international students can be a time-consuming process. Population statistics are not readily available from many parts of the world, and political factors can render carefully planned efforts ineffective overnight. Fortunately, a few resources are available. The *Directory of Overseas Educational Advising Centers* (College Board, 1985) lists the names and addresses of the United States Information Service (USIS) student advisers throughout the world. Statistical data about the current foreign student population in the United States is available in IIE's annual publication, *Open Doors* (Adams and others, 1984). Guidelines for the development of preadmissions materials are included among the wealth of information contained in a recruitment kit (available for cost) produced by the Foreign Student Recruitment Information Clearinghouse (National Liaison Committee . . . , 1985).

Summary

Recruitment of foreign students is a viable proposition when it is conducted in an ethical manner as a service to both the applicant and to the institution. Prior to embarking on such an endeavor, a self-evaluation of the institution's existing programs, facilities, and student support systems must be conducted and approval to host international students must be obtained from the Immigration and Naturalization Service. Staff for admissions, recruitment, and foreign student advising should be secured and trained. Target populations need to be defined in order to develop and disseminate preadmission materials designed for foreign audiences. Finally, the salient factor of an ethical recruitment program is the honest and accurate presentation of information to the prospective student.

References

Adams, E. A., Julian, A. C., and Laan, K. U. (eds). *Open Doors, 1983/84.* New York: Institute of International Education, 1984.

Brohm, J. F. "Recruiting Overseas: New Strategies for Overseas Representation." *NAFSA Newsletter,* 1980, *31* (6), 153-154.

College Board. *Directory of Overseas Educational Advising Centers.* New York: College Entrance Examination Board, 1985.

Goodwin, C. D., and Nacht, M. *Absence of Decision: Foreign Students in American Colleges and Universities.* New York: Institute of International Education, 1983.

Levitov, P. "Advising the Faculty on Specific Nationalities: Malaysian Students." *NAFSA Newsletter,* 1983, *35* (1), 11-12.

National Liaison Committee on Foreign Student Admissions. "Ethics Code to Stem Recruiting Abuses." *NAFSA Newsletter,* 1980a, *31* (7), 187-202.

National Liaison Committee on Foreign Student Admissions. *Foreign Student Recruitment: Realities and Recommendations.* New York: College Board, 1980b.

National Liaison Committee on Foreign Student Admissions. *Foreign Student Recruitment Information Clearinghouse Brochure.* Washington, D.C.: National Association for Foreign Student Affairs, 1984.

National Liaison Committee on Foreign Student Admissions. "Foreign Student Recruitment Kit." Washington, D.C.: Foreign Student Recruitment Information Clearinghouse, 1985.

Silney, J. "To Recruit or Not to Recruit?" *NAFSA Newsletter,* 1983, *35* (1), 9-10.

Mark D. Thackaberry is director of the International Student and Faculty Office at Northern Illinois University, DeKalb, Illinois.

Antoinette Liston is foreign student adviser at Southern Illinois University, Edwardsville, Illinois.

Assisting the foreign student to become a part of the total institution takes form in the student life area.

The Foreign Student and Student Life

Richard F. Reiff, Margaret A. Kidd

When a college or university accepts international students, it also accepts the responsibility to provide services and programs to meet their special needs and circumstances. To fulfill that responsibility, every institution enrolling international students should establish clearly written policies on international educational exchange. As stated in the "Standards and Responsibilities" of the National Association for Foreign Student Affairs (NAFSA): "Such policy must draw on and relate to the fundamental mission of the institution, recognize and direct sufficient resources for carrying out the policy, and carry the authority of the highest level in the institutional governance structure" (National Association . . . , 1979, p. 7). In addition to moral and ethical considerations, institutions have legal obligations regarding the admission and enrollment of international students. Most of these obligations relate to immigration regulations.

The services, programs, activities, and support services available to international students will have a significant impact on the quality of their educational experience. Cross-cultural adjustment and successful integration into campus life and the local community will result in a more meaningful experience for them. It will also contribute to a successful intercultural exchange program that is as beneficial to domestic students as to international students.

K R. Pyle (ed.). *Guiding the Development of Foreign Students.*
New Directions for Student Services, no. 36. San Francisco: Jossey-Bass, Winter 1986.

Virtually all programming for international students can be viewed in one of the following contexts: orientation, intercultural exchange, educational enrichment, or intercultural communication. Some programs are designed to facilitate adjustment, others to promote cultural exchange or facilitate the use of international students as educational resources. Some programs will fall into more than one category.

Prearrival Orientation

Orientation is essential to the cross-cultural adjustment of an international student. It should begin before the student leaves his or her home country. Many countries provide orientation programs that departing students should participate in. Programs providing general orientation to the United States and the system of education in the United States may be offered by the home country government, the binational commission United States Information Agency (USIA), or private institutions (such as the Hang Seng Bank in Hong Kong). Alumni groups are excellent resources for orientation to specific communities and campuses. Frequently, students returning home for vacations can be of assistance. Alumni groups and currently enrolled students should receive appropriate instruction and materials before offering orientation to new students.

The institution to which a student has been accepted should provide information about monetary requirements, health and accident insurance, immigration regulations, registration procedures, and local transportation. Information about housing assignments or available housing is vital to the arriving student. Whenever possible, new students should be met at the local bus terminal, train station, or airport and transported to their accommodations. Community volunteers, American students, and international students can function as greeters and can assist with transportation, housing, and orientation. Twenty-four-hour message centers are reassuring to students arriving from overseas. Staffed by volunteers or office personnel, message centers often operate around registration periods and can help arriving students coordinate unforeseen changes in travel plans. If housing is not arranged prior to arrival, experienced students and community volunteers can assist foreign students in locating suitable accommodations.

Campus Orientation

Every college or university that accepts international students should provide a comprehensive orientation program shortly after students arrive on campus. The orientation should (1) welcome new students and provide an opportunity for them to meet college or university staff and faculty, as well as community volunteers; (2) provide specific information to facilitate their adjustment to the campus; (3) increase their knowledge and understanding of the American system of higher education; (4) increase their understanding of American culture, values, and customs; and (5) impart some awareness of the impending cross-cultural adjustment process.

Orientation for international students can range from a half day to several weeks but should probably last at least two days. Orientation programs held on campus can be quite useful. Institutional staff and faculty can devote part of a day to orientees when the orientation is on campus. Campus facilities such as libraries, computer centers, recreational sports complexes, health centers, and laboratories are easily accessible. Budgets for on-campus orientations are generally smaller than for those held off campus.

Many successful orientation programs are also held off campus, where the undivided attention of students, faculty, and staff can be devoted to the program. Such orientation can create a sense of community among new international students as well as efficiently transmit valuable and necessary information.

A self-paced or do-it-yourself orientation may be appropriate if the number of new international students is small, the size of the staff or the budget is limited, or new students arrive at varying times to begin different academic programs.

The types of presentations included in any orientation program should be varied, and there should be frequent breaks. Presentations can include small lectures or group discussions, slide presentations, and films. Faculty and staff should participate to the extent possible. A business administration faculty member, for example, could lead a discussion on finances. Using experienced international and domestic students to lead small discussion groups can be very effective. The knowledge and perspective of these students are valuable and can serve as bridges between the presentations of faculty and staff and the realities of student life. For the purpose of small discussion groups, students can be divided according to culture or geographic regions if the number of students involved is adequate to permit division.

Before finalizing plans for an orientation program, certain factors should be considered. The level of English proficiency, degree of culture shock, cultural background, age, and academic objectives of the participants will affect the program's emphasis. Also, students that have very recently arrived in the United States may be suffering from jet lag and should not be expected to sit through long presentations.

Regardless of how the orientation is offered, it is important to cover topics that are necessary to students' initial adjustment and long-term well-being. Topics to include are best determined by the staff of the institution offering the program, but generally include advising and orientation procedures, community and campus services and programs, immigration regulations, finances (budgeting, banking, inflation), the system of education in the United States, and an introduction to intercultural communication. Every orientation should include a discussion of resource management. International students often have no idea of the wide variety and extent of human and material resources available to students at most colleges and universities in the United States. Many international students will be from countries in which institutions of higher education do not provide special departments and individuals to provide assistance with housing, finances, health services, and legal problems. International students should be made aware of these services, encouraged to take advantage of them, and shown how to use them.

Continuing Orientation

Continuing orientation programs can cover a broad range of topics, but should be developed according to specific objectives. Goals can best be determined by assessing students' needs for information. Some topics are of general interest to almost all students and the importance of these topics to the students on a particular campus will determine priority. Topics may include (1) health care in the United States, such as campus services, off-campus services, specialized care, emergency care, preventive health care, and medical and health insurance; (2) transportation and travel, such as local and public transportation, traveling nationally and internationally, and owning an automobile; (3) getting to know the region and its history, including cultural history, natural resources, local points of interest and ways to visit them; (4) how to see the United States, including regional descriptions, points of interest, economical transportation, and travel tips; (5) U.S. laws and the nonresident student, including immigration laws and regulations, federal and state tax laws, civil and criminal law, and sources of legal assistance; (6) interpersonal relationships, such as family life, dating, student-professor relationships, and intercultural communication; and (7) various aspects of American life, including the feminist movement, the peace movement, the antinuclear movement, environmentalism, and local and national election processes.

These and many other topics will be of interest and value to new international students during their adjustment to living in a new community. The expertise of campus and community members can be drawn upon for the presentations. An excellent format for continuing orientation programs is to follow the presentation with a discussion period and then a reception.

Programs for Intercultural Exchange

Programs for intercultural exchange promote interaction between cultures, increase awareness and understanding of other cultures, and provide information about specific elements of a culture, including values, customs, and beliefs. The goal of intercultural programs is to facilitate substantive international exchange, and every activity should have a specific purpose that will lead to this stated or implied goal. Programs that enhance understanding, awareness, open communication, and cultural sensitivity contribute to the personal development of students—both domestic and international. Programs that provide information or promote value clarification should be an integral part of students' education.

Substantive intercultural exchange can be best accomplished through well-planned, systematic, and purposeful programming. Merely bringing together students of different nationalities and cultures does not guarantee intercultural exchange or understanding. Research studies have shown that substantive interchange does not occur without some type of intervention or programming for international understanding. Failure to formulate clear goals and to plan activities accordingly only perpetuates cultural stereotypes (Riordan, 1978).

Although a broad range of programs and activities is desirable, the types, number, and frequency of international programs will depend on a variety of factors, including institutional size, foreign student population, human and material resources, community support, and institutional commitment to intercultural exchange. Some of these factors can be influenced, others cannot. For example, through a well-organized, systematic effort, community support can be increased. It may not, however, be possible to secure an increase in institutional funds for international activities. Careful assessment of the existing situation and conditions is a prerequisite to international programming.

The following programs are examples of some of the programming done on several college and university campuses. This is by no means an exhaustive list. Programming of this type is limited only by the creativity of the program planners and the care put into the planning process.

International Coffees. Coffees or teas can be a place to bring foreign students together with other foreign students, American students, international and American faculty, and community members for informal interaction and exchange. Interest in attending these gatherings will be enhanced if a series of coffees can be planned on a weekly or monthly schedule. The selection of a central, convenient location and a time when relatively few students are involved in classes or other work will also encourage attendance.

The international coffees should be well publicized through posters, student newspapers, housing publications, and radio. Publicity should emphasize that the event is for Americans and international students, that everyone is welcome, and that refreshments will be served.

Involving campus and community groups in the sponsorship and planning of international coffees is important for promoting continued interest in this type of programming. This cooperative effort can be achieved in a variety of ways. Campus or community civic, social, or religious organizations can be asked to sponsor a coffee by providing food and beverages. Members of the organization can also act as hosts by greeting guests as they arrive, interacting with them, and serving refreshments. Many organizations feel that encouraging international friendship and understanding is part of their mission and welcome the opportunity to meet this objective through sponsoring international events. International coffees are attractive to many organizations because they do not require a long-term commitment or great expense but provide an excellent opportunity for interaction.

International coffees should be relaxed and informal. Decorations and background music from other countries add to the global atmosphere. Beverages can include fruit punch and tea as well as coffee. Finger sandwiches, chips, fresh fruit, vegetables, cheeses, and cookies and other pastries are possible refreshments.

The purpose of the coffees is to encourage personal contact and interaction. The sponsoring groups may wish to make some welcoming remarks to introduce the guests to the organization and its interest in international events. A formal program, however, is rarely successful in this setting and can defeat the primary goals of contact and interaction.

International Talent Shows. Productions featuring songs, dances, instrumentals, fashion displays, skits, and poems of other countries provide an opportunity for individuals and groups from abroad to share the arts of their countries and cultures with the campus and community.

International student associations can plan the talent shows. Care should be taken to avoid overly long performances, ensure a variety of performances, and avoid disputes between groups. A planning committee representing the international student body and containing at least two staff or faculty members should consider all ideas and suggestions, view all proposed performances, and make decisions concerning which performances to include in the final program, the length of those performances, and the order in which they are presented.

Each act should last from three to six minutes, and the entire program should be no longer than two hours. Group dances with colorful costumes are particularly well received by audiences. It is important to ensure that the master of ceremonies, usually a foreign student, can be clearly understood by the audience and is accurately informed about each performance. International talent shows are annual events on many campuses.

International Exhibit Day. Exhibits featuring displays of arts, crafts, jewelry, and costumes brought by international students from their countries are a popular way to share these items of various cultures. Photograph and slide shows are often part of these exhibits, and, if campus policy permits, food samples can be given or sold to visitors. Foreign students from the countries represented should be available to answer questions about the displays. International exhibit day should be widely publicized on the campus and in the local community. Special invitations can be sent to local elementary and secondary schools, where international exhibit day is particularly popular and very effective in promoting cultural exchange.

International Documentary Film Nights. A film night featuring three to five short documentary films from different countries usually sparks interest and leads to lively discussion. International students can be responsible for selecting and introducing the films and for answering questions following each film. A variety of films are available from embassies or consulates, often without charge to students.

Although students should play a major role in selecting films for this program, the international student adviser or other appropriate staff or faculty member should preview each film to ensure that it is appropriate for international documentary film night. Films with a clearly commercial message may not be appropriate.

Discussion Groups. Group discussions are an effective and interesting format for the exchange of ideas on topics of mutual concern. Groups should be relatively small (not to exceed twenty students) and should include international and American students. Although no formal preparation is necessary, someone should be designated to lead the discussion. The leader could be someone with particular skills in facilitating group discussion, someone with specific experience or knowledge related to the topic of discussion, or merely someone interested in leading a discussion on a particular topic.

Discussions can include such topics as family life, religion, sex roles, childrearing, and other aspects of society in various cultures. Topics selected by students will promote interest and an informal, relaxed atmosphere will encourage participation in the discussion.

International Events Forums. Forums are an excellent opportunity for students to gain understanding and firsthand knowledge of significant international events. For example, students from Lebanon discussing politics in that country will add relevance to what American and other students have heard and read. However, foreign students should not be pressured to discuss topics that might be threatening or uncomfortable for them.

Forums also combine international programming efforts with academic interests. A forum can be easily incorporated into classes that combine content with experience. International students can serve on a panel to answer questions relevant to such topics as history, sociology, political science, international business, and foreign relations. Forums in which students from different countries discuss their experiences as students in the United States are also interesting and educational.

International Week. A week-long campus-wide event can include a number of the programs and activities already mentioned. Programs and activities can provide specific information and cross-cultural experiences that will enhance awareness, sensitivity, and understanding and can help to meet the more general objective of promoting cultural exchange and international goodwill on college or university campuses.

Foreign students should be primarily responsible for the planning and implementation of international programs. An international film festival or an evening highlighting the arts, culture, history, and development of a specific country could be a part of this special week. Students should be encouraged to contact their embassies or consulates for assistance. Nationality groups on other campuses can often share information about their successes and failures in preparing for such events. The profile of international week will be determined to a great extent by student interest, institutional support, available campus and community resources, and the creative application of those resources.

An ideal way to begin international week is with an introductory speech by a keynote speaker of international renown or a speaker with recognized expertise in an area of international interest.

Campus Friend Program. This program matches a foreign student and an American student and is designed to help new students from abroad become oriented to the college or university and to promote ongoing intercultural exchange. American students who volunteer for this program should be oriented in the cultural differences and aspects of intercultural communication. Although most of the activities are determined by the students themselves, some special activities designed to promote intercultural communication and understanding should be conducted by the international student adviser. Potluck dinners, excursions, cross-cultural simulation games, and role-playing exercises are helpful activities for the participants. American students will often invite their campus friend home for the holidays. Other activities include having meals together, attending campus programs together, and visiting places of mutual interest. The relationship of campus friends and the kinds of experiences they are sharing should be periodically assessed.

Community Friend/Host Family Program. This is considered by many professionals in campus-based international programs to be one of the most effective ways of promoting substantive cultural exchange in the community. This program matches an international student with an American family or friend who provides occasional hospitality to the international student. The American family or friend includes the student in a variety of activities that routinely occur, such as dinners, shopping trips, and excursions. This program is an excellent way for the international student to learn about life within the context of the family in the United States. For many international students, it is their only opportunity to observe American family life.

A mandatory orientation for both students and families should be an integral part of this program. Written materials are very helpful to both students and families, and culture-specific materials should be provided whenever possible. Students and families alike will enjoy discovering how they differ from cultural stereotypes and which ways they conform.

The relationship of the international student and the host family should be periodically monitored to ensure that the goals of the program are being met and to attempt to divert difficulties that will inevitably arise in even the most capably directed programs.

International Speakers' Bureau. Another program that can be directed by a community group is a speakers' bureau, although it can just as successfully be coordinated by the international student adviser. The speakers' bureau arranges opportunities for international students who have volunteered to present programs about their country or some aspect of their culture. Topics might include education, government, natural resources, sex roles, family life, and religion. Some international students will have slides, films, costumes, or photographs to enhance their presentations. Other students will want to talk about various aspects of their career interest as it is practiced in their country.

The speakers' bureau should be well publicized in the community so that interested groups such as schools, churches, and civic groups will be aware of this service and how to use it. A brochure describing the program, with a list of countries and suggested topics, could be sent to appropriate campus and community organizations.

International students should be carefully selected for the speakers' bureau. Their qualifications, such as English language proficiency, speaking ability, time availability, and knowledge of topics, should be considered. Those selected for the speakers' bureau should receive written guidelines, an orientation, and training before they speak before groups.

The speakers' bureau presents an excellent opportunity for international students to share their culture with Americans. Participation gives students a sense of identity and importance and is an ideal way to promote global understanding and goodwill.

Educational Enrichment

Learning from and with international students will engender interest in intercultural exchange. International students are effective educational resources in both formal and informal settings. Faculty and staff are often unaware of the many opportunities for advanced learning and personal growth that exist through interaction with international students. Through in-service training programs, presentations at departmental meetings, written materials, and personal contacts, international student advisers can make faculty and staff aware of the educational resource value of international students. Developing incentives and rewards for faculty that use international students as educational resources has been effective in some institutions.

Oregon has developed and implemented a statewide program using international students as resources in the public schools throughout the state and in government agencies, businesses, and industries within the state. The program is funded by the state and provides a tuition benefit for participating students. Supervision is centered in the Office of Academic Affairs, Oregon State System of Higher Education, and administered by the international office on the campus of each of the five participating institutions.

Helpful resources on utilizing international students include Josef Mestenhauser's book, *Learning with Foreign Students,* and the film *Personalizing the Educational Process: Internationals as Human Resources,* produced by Richard F. Reiff.

Programs for Intercultural Communication

Intercultural communication programs are related to nonverbal, oral, or written communication and other aspects of human communication patterns that vary among people of different cultures. The most popular form for this type of program is the intercultural communication workshop (ICW). The ICW traditionally includes simulation games, role playing, case studies, and intercultural communication exercises.

Participants in ICWs should include domestic as well as international students. International students should ideally have been in the United States for six to twelve months. ICWs should be led by experienced facilitators; such programs often do not achieve expected results when led by novices. Most colleges and universities have experienced faculty or professional staff who can be called on to lead such workshops.

An excellent reference for developing intercultural communication programs is Gary Althen's book, *Learning Across Cultures.*

Conclusion

The presence of international students on the campus creates both challenges and opportunities. When an institution accepts a student, it is obligated to fulfill certain needs and to make opportunities for personal growth and development available. When it accepts international students, it is obligated to consider their special needs when planning programs and activities.

The presence of students from diverse cultures creates opportunities for cross-cultural learning for domestic students. This may be the first opportunity for cross-cultural contact that many domestic students have.

It is worth repeating, for emphasis, that such contact may perpetuate cultural stereotypes rather than provide the desired substantive intercultural exchange if objectives have not been carefully formulated. The programs presented in this chapter should be viewed as a springboard to develop programs consistent with institutional policies and resources.

References

Althen, G. (ed.). *Learning Across Cultures: Intercultural Communication and International Educational Exchange.* Washington, D.C.: National Association for Foreign Student Affairs, 1981.

Mestenhauser, J. A. *Learning with Foreign Students.* Minneapolis: University of Minnesota, 1976.

National Association for Foreign Student Affairs. *Standards and Responsibilities in International Educational Interchange: Guideline Series I.* Washington, D.C.: National Association for Foreign Student Affairs, 1979.

Reiff, R. F. (producer). *Personalizing the Educational Process: Internationals as Human Resources* (film). Washington, D.C.: National Association for Foreign Student Affairs, 1975.

Riordan, C. "Developing Tolerance: A Comparison of Contextual vs. Program Effects." *International Journal of Intercultural Relations,* 1978, 2, 309–327.

Richard F. Reiff is director of the Office of International Services and Programs, University of Georgia. He has been active in international student affairs since 1970 and is a former vice president for regional affairs of the National Association for Foreign Student Affairs.

Margaret A. Kidd is director of the International Office of the University of Texas at Austin. The International Office provides educational support services for foreign students and faculty in the United States and for American students and faculty studying and working in other countries.

*Advising and counseling international students require
awareness of the adaptation period experienced by sojourners
in a foreign country, sensitivity to the powerful impact of
culture on behavior, and willingness to empathize with the
value systems of international students.*

Advising and Counseling the International Student

Ron A. J. Cadieux, Bea Wehrly

Mr. Kim has been in the United States at a large university on the West
Coast for two months. On arriving in the United States he decided that he
did not want to interact with other Korean students but instead wanted to
make American friends. Unfortunately, Mr. Kim has been unable to go
beyond superficial acquaintanceships with any American students. He is
puzzled by how Americans develop friendships and at times feels that
Americans do not want to get to know a student from another country.

Mr. Ramirez is a recently arrived undergraduate student from Mexico. Although his spoken English is quite good, he is very worried about
his writing ability. This is his first quarter in the United States. His adviser
recommends that he take a mathematics and a chemistry course to com-
plement his interest in an engineering major. University regulations dic-
tate that he also take courses in the social sciences and humanities.

What is the adviser's or counselor's role in assisting international
students such as Mr. Kim and Mr. Ramirez who find themselves in difficult
situations? What do professionals need to know about adaptation in order
to effectively advise and counsel students in these situations? What are
some guidelines that will help advisers and counselors handle these and
other situations?

K R. Pyle (ed.). *Guiding the Development of Foreign Students.*
New Directions for Student Services, no. 36. San Francisco: Jossey-Bass, Winter 1986.

International Students' Unique Advising Needs

When international students are asked to prioritize their goals in coming to the United States, the majority will indicate that the largest percentage of their time and energy is directed towarding achieving academic goals (Cadieux, 1983). Academic advising is, therefore, a critical activity.

In some respects, international students encounter the same academic problems as their American counterparts. Concern about whether they will succeed academically, whether they have chosen the right school, and about developing good rapport with fellow students and professors is common. International students, however, have a number of unique concerns. Storey (1982) has discussed the inadequate and culturally bound nature of contemporary student development theories as they relate to international students.

As Bulthuis (Chapter Two of this volume) acknowledges, Lee, Abd-Ella, and Burks (1981) found that five of the most common concerns reported by international students from developing countries were language difficulties, financial problems, adjustment to a new educational system, social and cultural adjustment, and relevance of academic programs.

Language Difficulties. Ability to speak the language is by far the most prevailing concern that international students have about their educational experience in the United States. A lack of English language proficiency will affect students' ability to accomplish reading assignments; express opinions in class where discussion is encouraged; understand lectures, instructions, and notices; and answer essay questions in examinations. Lack of English language proficiency will also inhibit the extent of their contact with professors as well as with their fellow students.

The case of Mr. Ramirez cited at the beginning of this chapter is not altogether uncommon. Language proficiency is generally an important issue when an international student first arrives and takes a nontechnical course. In a case such as this an adviser would be wise to direct a student to a course requiring very little writing.

Financial Problems. The second most commonly expressed concern of international students is the lack of sufficient funds. The assumption that most international students come from wealthy backgrounds or have access to more than sufficient funds for their education is erroneous. Financial stress affects students' academic life by consuming their emotional energy as well as by prompting students to take heavier academic loads in order to graduate as soon as possible. This drive toward accelerated academic progress may not always be in a student's best interest.

Adjusting to a New Educational System. The difference between the educational system of the student's country and that of the United States is often quite dramatic. International students must quickly come to terms with these differences if they are to be academically successful. For example, international students are generally accustomed to being tested on material that they have memorized. In American classrooms students are expected to synthesize material covered in class for the purpose of formulating their own ideas. Another area of adjustment is the format of questions asked on examinations; multiple choice questions are often unfamiliar and therefore difficult for international students, since this test format is not frequently used in other countries. Also, international students are usually accustomed to following a set curriculum rather than one with a choice of coursework. Choosing their own courses, in conjunction with a greater breadth of material covered in classes, are differences that challenge international students.

Social and Cultural Adjustment. Other areas of difficulty in academic adjustment relate to interpersonal communication with faculty, administrators, and fellow students. Generally, international students come from environments in which the nature of student-to-student interaction is cooperative. It is often difficult for them to become accustomed to the competition among students in their new environment. International students generally expect a formal relationship with professors and are often puzzled by the relaxed, unassuming posture taken by many faculty. Oral class participation expected in many courses, such as participating in discussion and asking questions in class, can also be a new educational experience.

Relevance of Academic Programs. The issue of academic relevance is noted as being an important concern among international students. Educators cannot assume that international students' educational needs are the same as their U.S. counterparts. International students come from educational and cultural backgrounds that differ greatly from the U.S. system. When they return to their countries, they are expected to apply their education to their home culture. American higher education may fall short of meeting these students' needs. International students must constantly struggle to translate their new knowledge into an appropriate context for their home setting.

Guidelines for Advisers

The duties of advisers of international students are not completely different from advising responsibilities for U.S. students. Both student groups have similar needs. However, international students' perspectives and unique experiences demand special consideration.

Most international students regard academic advising as a very important service (Lee, Abd-Ella, and Burks, 1981). An international student's academic adviser may be the most important and influential person he or she encounters in the United States. Althen (1981) maintains that effective cross-cultural advising requires an awareness of culture's influence on the way people think, feel, and act and that advisers must be concerned with their own attitudes, knowledge, and skills. Poor advising is often the cause for students dropping out or transferring (Palmer, 1984). Weill (1982) contends that advising international students involves considerably more time than is normally required to advise American students.

One of the first dimensions to consider in advising international students is developing rapport. Before undertaking this task, it is important for an adviser to become familiar with a student's situation. Advisers often are not aware of the complexities of cross-cultural education and may not understand the emotionalism and dynamics of cross-cultural learning. Hood and Schieffer (1984) recommend that advisers become familiar with international students' cultures and academic backgrounds, that there be regular contact between adviser and advisee, and that advisers become acquainted with work opportunities in the students' home countries.

Social interaction can also be very helpful in establishing rapport. Most international students are intensely curious about social and family customs in the United States. Invitations extended to students by advisers to social functions, particularly those of a family nature, will usually be welcomed.

An international student's academic level must be determined by the academic adviser soon after the student's arrival. The adviser must make the decision regarding how the student's academic preparation meshes with the curriculum of the university. The importance of fitting the student into the university curriculum cannot be overemphasized. Enrolling students in courses that they do not need wastes time and money and may lead to poor study habits and students' poor opinion of their advisers' judgments. In addition, placing students in courses for which they are inadequately prepared leads to poor grades and low morale.

Another important dimension of an academic adviser's role is to recommend the course load that a student should undertake. Generally, a rule of thumb is to consider the student's academic record in conjunction with the difficulty of the proposed coursework. As previously mentioned, English language proficiency is a vitally important variable to consider when advising international students. This is particularly true when a student is enrolled in courses requiring extensive reading or writing. Some international students who have had superior academic success in their home countries may have unrealistic expectations of themselves in the United States. Helping students arrive at realistic goals requires patience and sensitive advising.

Although most international students are hampered by English language difficulties, this does not prevent the majority of them from succeeding. The academic adviser can do much to assist those who are experiencing either an initial or prolonged struggle with the English language. Such ideas as enrolling in an English-as-a-second-language course, recommending a reduced course load, and assisting the student in locating tutors are areas in which an academic adviser can provide valuable assistance. Some universities have writing centers and are able to help international students with their writing skills. Advisers can also encourage American students to work closely with international students. Advisers can also assist students by critiquing their papers and by taking the time to explain errors in English language usage.

Providing complementary learning opportunities is of particular importance for international students. Upon returning home, many of these students move quickly into positions of responsibility. Complementary experiences help international students make the link between their academic learning and the practical reality of the working world. Advisers can greatly facilitate learning by encouraging and assisting in planning experiences, such as practicums, internships, and postdegree training programs.

It is also important for advisers of international students to encourage their participation in nonacademic activities such as student and campus organizations as well as social and cultural events. These students are also a tremendous educational resource to the campus community for their ability to educate the campus population toward greater understanding of other cultures as well as exposing them to different perspectives on international events. Academic advisers can find out international students' interests in making such contributions and may assist in arranging talks, panel presentations, and other public forums.

Finally, academic advisers of international students need to serve as their advocates within the university community. A significant portion of any university community is not aware of the unique circumstances and needs of the international students. This can be ameliorated by consciously attempting to educate faculty and staff about this student population and the way to work most effectively with them.

Special Areas of Competence for Advisers. There are a number of professional qualities and areas of competence that must be emphasized for academic advisers. The first relates to advisers' knowledge of educational systems in other countries. It is very difficult to understand the academic direction a student might want to follow unless an adviser is familiar with that student's background. This educational process on the part of the adviser may take considerable time and energy. Certainly, much of this information can be gleaned from the student but it must also be supplemented by reference materials that compare educational systems between other countries and the United States. Integrating the educational experiences of international students in their own countries with the requirements and objectives of programs in which these students are enrolled in American institutions will assist the adviser in helping students adjust to a new academic system and in planning appropriate academic agendas.

Assisting students to appreciate academic relevance is a second area where advisers can provide assistance. The application of learning is an extremely important matter of concern for international students. A student's primary interest in studying in the United States is often the acquisition of knowledge and skills that can be utilized in his or her country. Not all aspects of any academic program will be meeting the specific needs of a particular student's situation. However, an academic adviser's prudent guidance can be a vital variable in assisting students to better satisfy their academic needs.

A successful adviser of international students also needs to be very aware of the special concerns of this student population. Concern about language proficiency, adjustment to the U.S. educational system, relevance of programs, finances, and social and cultural adjustment should be considered in every adviser's interaction with an international student. Sensitivity to these issues will greatly enhance an adviser's effectiveness in working with this population.

Third, an effective adviser of international students is a person who constantly strives to remain flexible and open to cultural differences. This attribute is one that must continue to be developed. An academic adviser is one of the most important and influential persons an international student will encounter in the United States. To be effective, advisers must understand and accept these students.

Counseling International Students

There is no clear line that distinguishes the tasks of advising and counseling international students. Advisers of foreign students recognize that international students sometimes need specialized help from counselors. The trauma of adjusting to a vastly different culture is increased by the pressure of trying to function while coping with a foreign language. The ongoing vulnerabilty felt by most non-Western international students during their sojourn in the United States has been documented by numerous researchers (Alexander and others, 1981; Domingues, 1970; Meleis, 1982; Penn and Durham, 1978; Pruitt, 1978; Stafford, Marion, and Salter, 1980).

Among the problems faced by international students that may necessitate the specialized services of cross-cultural counseling are loneliness and homesickness, loss of status and identify, fear of failure, depression, and somatic symptoms (Alexander and others, 1981; Sook, 1984; Dillard and Chisolm, 1983; Meleis, 1982; Pruitt, 1978; Stafford, Marian, and Salter, 1980; Shiow-Huey, 1984). Loneliness and homesickness are common problems faced by international students. These problems may reach crisis proportions if a foreign student is unable to find ongoing support from conational or American peers. Loss of status and identity and feelings of worthlessness may ensue for students who feel they have left their identity behind and are groping for an identity in a culture they do not understand.

Pressure to succeed and fear of failure are especially strong among non-Western students, for whom identification with the family is paramount (Althen and Stott, 1983). Not to succeed in academic endeavors abroad can bring enormous shame to foreign students and to their families. This burden of shame can become unbearable for some international students who are not living up to their own academic expectations.

Depression is a symptom commonly experienced by international students as they simultaneously cope with cultural shock and heavy academic loads. Manifestations of depression differ, however, and appear to be influenced by culture (Binitie, 1975; Kleinman, 1980; Kleinman and Good, 1985; Marsella, 1980; Marsella, Kinzie, and Gordon, 1973; Marsella and others, 1975). This makes diagnosis and treatment of depression particularly challenging for the counselor working with students of other cultures.

International students' emotional problems may evolve into physical problems. Alexander and others (1981) studied the use of the University of Wisconsin health services by all students and found that, while overall use of health services by non-Western international students was about the same as by American students, the types of complaints that international students brought to the health service were different. Non-Western international students brought more gastrointestinal, generalized and undifferentiated, psychosomatic, and pain-related complaints than did American and Western students. Students who repeatedly suffer from gastrointestinal problems may be suffering from depression.

Challenges for Counselors

In a stratified sampling of international students from seventy-five countries, Dadfar and Friedlander (1982) found that European and Latin students held considerably more positive viewpoints toward seeking professional psychological help than did Asian and African students. Minimal use of university counseling services by non-Western students supports these findings. Many non-Western students are reluctant to seek help from professional counselors for emotional problems. Their reluctance may stem from their cultural belief system that considers it a shame and stigma for the family to seek help outside the family. Religious and philosophical belief systems may also discourage the use of Western counseling systems.

An Asian student suffering from strain in her first year on an American campus ended up being hospitalized for stomach ulcers. The student refused to go for help at the university's counseling center and chose to rely on the support of conationals. The student did recover and suffered no debilitating ulcer attacks during the subsequent three years of her undergraduate program in the United States.

Expectations of treatment may vary greatly among international students when they do turn to a counseling center for help (Tan, 1967; Yuen and Tinsley, 1981). Foreign students from authoritarian cultures may expect the counseling session to be directive in format and may be confused by the absence of direct advice from some counselors.

Students' preferences for formal versus informal settings for the counseling sessions can also vary. They may expect a formal relationship with the counselor, who is viewed as an expert, and the relaxed atmosphere of many higher education counseling centers in the United States and the informal demeanor of many counselors may be contrary to all expectations. As a result, the credibility of such services may suffer in the perceptions of some international students.

Counseling, as practiced in most higher education counseling centers in the United States, is very Western in orientation and not always geared to understanding the needs of non-Western students (Alexander and others, 1981; Johnson, 1984; O'Brien, 1984; Pratomthong and Baker, 1983; Pederson and others, 1981; Sue, 1985; Wehrly, in press; Wehrly and Deen, 1983; Wehrly and Watson-Gegeo, 1985). Western-style counseling techniques that emphasize self-disclosure may be viewed as an invasion of privacy and a violation of cultural norms. Emphasis on the self as the central focus in all decision making also contradicts many non-Western traditional value systems in which the family is the central focus in decision making (Okon, 1983; Rhee, 1985).

Perceptions of helping processes and understandings of the causes and solutions of problems are rooted in the value systems of the culture in which a student is socialized. Thinking processes are influenced by culture. Counselors working with students from other cultures must be aware that students may be perceiving problems and resolutions from a vastly different framework than that of the counselor.

Counselors should be aware of the variations among cultures of acceptable ways to express mental anguish. One Asian American counselor working with a Puerto Rican client considered it important to help her client stop crying during the counseling sessions and taught the client deep-breathing techniques to achieve this. The counselor was imposing her value of a stoic expression of unhappiness on the Puerto Rican client, whose culture accepts a more open expression of feelings.

Cross-cultural communication skills are important for counselors who face language barriers, nonverbal communication differences, and clients' needs for culture-specific information on value systems. Students communicate nonverbally as well, through such behavior as physical distance, eye contact, gestures, and silence. A Japanese student who smiles throughout the counseling session and an African student who has difficulty maintaining eye contact and looks at the floor during most of the session may be indicating nothing more than respect for the counselor. Contradictions in findings on nonverbal behavior in different cultures make interpreting nonverbal behavior especially challenging for counselors of foreign students (Vogelaar and Silverman, 1984).

Guidelines for Counselors

A paramount criterion for effective counseling across cultures is a heightened awareness of one's own culture and the danger of ethnocentric attitudes when working with people from other cultures (Sue, 1985; Wehrly, in press). Stewart (1972) has proposed a four-dimensional paradigm to examine the impact of culture on oneself, which examines a person's forms of activity, forms of social relations, perceptions of the world, and perceptions of the self and the individual. Such self study can help counselors realize the cultural "loading" of assumptions that each person develops, but rarely examines, in the process of socialization. Self study can also reduce the number of cultural blind spots in the helping process.

Counselors need to examine not only the influence of their cultural heritage on their world views but also any biases or buried feelings they may have against persons of a particular culture. Hidden anger can be extremely damaging in the cross-cultural helping relationship (Kleinman, 1985). A counselor who has had a negative experience with a person from a particular culture may find negative feelings surfacing each time he or she comes in contact with students of that culture. Counselors must recognize these feelings and identify their origins in order to avoid acting on them in a negative way during subsequent cross-cultural counseling.

The counselor who works with international students must be willing to learn with and from each international student that he or she counsels. To avoid stereotyping, the unique value system of each individual must be understood, especially those qualities that are unique to a given culture. Determining whether cultural differences are part of the counselee's problem is crucial if the counselor is to avoid stereotyping the counselee. Counselor sterotypes are very damaging to the counseling relationship since, at best, they are usually considered demeaning and may even be viewed as an insult by the counselee. Stewart (1981) proposes a model of cross-cultural counseling based on empathy that understands both similarities and differences in cultures.

Development of rapport with counselees is of paramount importance for international student counselors. For many international students, sharing personal problems with a stranger is looked on with trepidation, and it is important to develop trust before counseling can commence. Ideally, international student counselors are active in orientation programs for international students so that they know of this option as soon as they reach the campus. Counselors who work with international students must be willing to spend much time with these students outside of the formal setting of the counseling office, for these informal meetings can be very helpful. Working with international friendship clubs, attending special holiday and cultural programs put on by various international student groups, being available in food-service settings patronized by international students, as well as being willing to be present when these students meet with their academic advisers are some ways counselors can indicate willingness to be friends who care enough to go beyond cultural barriers to gain more understanding. Being known as a caring person in this way can greatly aid a counselor's work with international students.

The following suggestions for building bridges across the cultures of the counselor and counselee are adapted from suggestions made by the medical anthropologist, Arthur Kleinman (1985):

1. Work to develop a relationship built on mutual trust. During this process the counselor enlists the help of foreign students to learn how they define their problems, what these problems mean to them, and how these problems impact their daily lives. Counselees are encouraged to tell how the problems bother them, how serious they think the problems are, when the problems started, what they believe caused their problems, and how they think they can be helped. Kleinman calls these "explanatory models" (Kleinman, 1980) and describes in detail the rationale and procedures for incorporating these as part of the cross-cultural helping process.

2. Help the counselee determine if cultural clashes are part of the problem the counselee is facing. This process includes enlisting the international student's aid in educating the counselor about cultural value systems that seem to impinge on the student's problems.

3. Work with counselees to help them determine the values they can live with during this time when they are required to function in more than one cultural value system. Again, the counselor and counselee effort is a joint one in which the counselor will be a learner as well as a teacher.

4. Help counselees choose and implement behavior with which they feel comfortable. These choices must be based on the results of the value systems clarification engaged in during Step 3.

Kleinman recognizes that the partnership efforts described in Steps 1 through 4 may at first be very foreign to the non-Western counselee, since these students may expect to be told what is wrong with them and how to solve their problems. However, Kleinman assures those of us in the helping professions that based on his own experience it is possible to work successfully in this manner. The authors of this chapter have also found these partnership endeavors to be useful processes in cross-cultural counseling.

Counselor roles may also include working with the international student counselees as change agents in the cultural milieus in which these foreign students operate. Such change agent roles must, however, be undertaken with much sensitivity to the cultural pride of the counselees. As an example, direct confrontation can do almost irreparable harm to an individual from a culture where saving face is important, and it is rarely used for problem resolution in such cultures.

An ongoing change agent role for foreign student counselors is to help build and strengthen networks and support groups among other international students and with supportive U.S. nationals. This effort should begin when the international student first arrives on campus. Serving as a catalyst in faculty development workshops to help broaden cross-cultural teaching skills is another important role for the counselor as change agent (Shana'a, 1978; Vigushin, 1982). Faculty development seminars may include using a variety of techniques in which there are small lectures as well as active involvement in simulations and interaction among the faculty and foreign students (Fiedler, Mitchell, and Triandis, 1971; Vigushin, 1982).

In summary, the following counselor qualities are very important for effective counseling with international students:

- Cultural self-awareness and sensitivity
- Awareness of assumptions and values of both the counselor and counselee that underlie the counseling process
- Openness to and respect for differing value systems
- Tolerance for ambiguity
- Willingness to learn with and from counselees
- Genuine care and concern for people with differing value systems.

References

Alexander, A. A., Klein, M. H., Workneh, F., and Miller, M. H. "Psychotherapy and the Foreign Student." In P. B. Pedersen, J. G. Draguns, W. J. Lonner, and J. E. Trimble (eds.), *Counseling Across Cultures.* Honolulu: University Press of Hawaii, 1981.

Althen, G., (ed.). *Learning Across Cultures: Intercultural Communication and International Educational Exchange.* Washington, D.C.: The National Association for Foreign Student Affairs, 1981.

Althen, G., and Stott, F. W., "Advising and Counseling Students Who Have Unrealistic Academic Objectives." *The Personnel and Guidance Journal,* 1983, *61* (10), 608-611.

Binitie, A. "A Factor-Analytical Study of Depression Across Cultures (African and European)." *British Journal of Psychiatry,* 1975, *127,* 559-563.

Cadieux, R. "An Exploratory Study of the Adaptive Process Among Selected Korean Students at Michigan State University." Unpublished doctoral dissertation, Department of Higher Education Administration, Michigan State University, 1983.

Dillard, J. M., and Chisolm, G. B. "Counseling the International Student in a Multicultural Context." *Journal of College Student Personnel,* 1983, *24* (2), 101-105.

Domingues, P. M. "Student Personnel Services for International Students." *Journal of NAWDAC,* 1970, *33* (2), 83-89.

Fiedler, F. E., Mitchell, T., and Triandis, H. C. "The Cultural Assimilator: An Approach to Cross-Cultural Training." *Journal of Applied Psychology,* 1971, *55* (2), 95-102.

Hood, M. A., and Schieffer, K. J. (eds.). *Professional Integration: A Guide for Stu-*

dents from the Developing World. Washington, D.C.: National Association for Foreign Student Affairs, 1984.

Johnson, J. Personal communication, July 26, 1984.

Kleinman, A. *Patients and Healers in the Context of Culture.* Berkeley: University of California Press, 1980.

Kleinman, A. "Cross-Cultural Psychotherapeutic Practice." Keynote address, the Third Annual Teachers College Roundtable for Cross-Cultural Counseling and Psychotherapy, New York, N.Y., February 22, 1985.

Kleinman, A., and Good, B. (eds.). *Culture and Depression.* Berkeley: University of California Press, 1985.

Lee, M. Y., Abd-Ella, M., and Burks, L. A. *Needs of Foreign Students from Developing Nations at U.S. Colleges and Universities.* Washington, D.C.: National Association for Foreign Student Affairs, 1981.

Marsella, A. J. "Depressive Experience and Disorder Across Cultures." In H. C. Triandis and J. G. Draguns (eds.), *Handbook of Cross-Cultural Psychology,* vol. 6. Newton, Mass.: Allyn and Bacon, 1980.

Marsella, A. J., Kinzie, D., and Gordon, P. "Ethnic Variations in the Expression of Depression." *Journal of Cross-Cultural Psychology,* 1973, *4* (4), 435-459.

Marsella, A. J., Sanborn, K. O., Kameoka, V., Shizum, L., and Brennan, J. "Cross-Validation of Self-Report Measures of Depression Among Normal Populations of Japanese, Chinese, and Caucasian Ancestry." *Journal of Clinical Psychology,* 1975, *31* (2), 281-287.

Meleis, A. I. "Arab Students in Western Universities." *Journal of Higher Education,* 1982, *53* (4), 439-447.

O'Brien, C. R. Personal communication, July 26, 1984.

Okon, S. "Guidance and Counseling in Nigeria." *The Personnel and Guidance Journal,* 1983, *61* (8), 457-458.

Palmer, S. E. "Advice on Academic Advising: Faculty Members May Face Increasing Pressure to Help Students." *Chronicle of Higher Education,* 1984, *2,* 25.

Pedersen, P. B., Draguns, J. G., Lonner, W. J., and Trimble, J. E. (eds.). *Counseling Across Cultures.* Honolulu: University Press of Hawaii, 1981.

Penn, R. J., and Durham, M. L. "Dimensions of Cross-Cultural Interaction." *Journal of College Student Personnel,* 1978, *19* (3), 264-267.

Pratomthong, S. J., and Baker, S. B. "Overcoming Obstacles to the Growth and Development of Guidance and Counseling in Thailand." *The Personnel and Guidance Journal,* 1983, *61* (8), 466-469.

Pruitt, F. J. "The Adaptation of Foreign Students on American Campuses," *Journal of NAWDAC,* 1978, *41* (4), 144-147.

Rhee, S. Personal communication, October 6, 1985.

Shana'a, J. "The Foreign Student: Better Understanding for Better Teaching." *Improving College and University Teaching,* 1978, *26* (4), 243-246.

Shiow-Huey Wang. Personal communication, July 25, 1984.

Sook Hee Chun. Personal communication, July 24, 1984.

Stafford, T. H., Marion, P. B., and Salter, M. L. "Adjustment of International Students." *NASPA Journal,* 1980, *18* (1), 40-45.

Stewart, E. C. *American Cultural Patterns: A Cross-Cultural Perspective.* Yarmouth, Maine: Intercultural Press, 1972.

Stewart, E. C. "Cultural Sensitivities in Counseling." In P. B. Pedersen, J. G. Draguns, W. J. Lonner, and J. E. Trimble (eds.), *Counseling Across Cultures.* Honolulu: University Press of Hawaii, 1981.

Story, K. E. "The Student Development Professional and the Foreign Student: A Conflict of Values." *Journal of College Student Personnel,* 1982, *23* (1), 66-70.

Sue, D. W. "The Counselor of Tommorow: A Multicultural Perspective." *ACES Newsletter*, 1985, *44* (4), 11-12.

Tan, H. "Intercultural Study of Counseling Expectancies." *Journal of Counseling Psychology*, 1967, *14* (2), 122-130.

Vigushin, J. "Helping Campus Personnel Help Foreign Students: A Counseling Simulation." *The Humanist Educator*, 1982, *20* (3), 134-142.

Vogelaar, L.M.E., and Silverman, M. "Nonverbal Communication in Crosscultural Counseling: A Literature Review." *International Journal for the Advancement of Counseling*, 1984, *7* (1), 41-57.

Wehrly, B. "Counseling International Students—Issues, Concerns, and Programs." *International Journal for the Advancement of Counseling*, in press.

Wehrly, B., and Deen, N. "Counseling and Guidance Issues from a Worldwide Perspective: An Introduction." *The Personnel and Guidance Journal*, 1983, *61* (8), 452.

Wehrly, B., and Watson-Gegeo, K. "Ethnographic Methodologies as Applied to the Study of Cross-Cultural Counseling." In P. Pedersen (ed.), *Handbook of Cross-Cultural Counseling and Therapy*. Westport, Conn.: Greenwood Press, 1985.

Weill, L. V. "Advising International Students at Small Colleges." *NACADA Journal*, 1982, *2* (1), 52-56.

Yuen, R.K.W., and Tinsley, H.E.A. "International and American Students' Expectancies about Counseling." *Journal of Counseling Psychology*, 1981, *28* (1), 66-69.

Ron A. J. Cadieux is presently management education coordinator at Riverside Methodist Hospital, Columbus, Ohio. Previously, he was Coordinator of International Student Advising at Ohio State University, Columbus.

Bea Wehrly is professor of counselor education at Western Illinois University, Macomb. She is a past chairperson of the International Relations Committee of the American Association of Counseling and Development.

A review of the research literature on foreign students gives us insight into approaches and programs that have potential for success.

Research on Foreign Students at Colleges and Universities in the United States

Paul B. Marion

Since the time of the Greeks, "scholars and students have traveled to the intellectually dominant countries in search of knowledge" (Pruitt, 1978, p. 144). Students from other countries have been coming to the United States since 1784, according to Hendricks and Skinner (1977), and the number has increased tremendously since the end of World War II. This increase is due to the importance of the United States as a leading industrial nation, of the English language as the primary world language, the high quality of higher education in the United States, the availability of good jobs in the United States, unstable political and economic conditions in many other countries, and the availability of scholarship funds.

American colleges and universities have generally encouraged foreign students to enroll in order to encourage international understanding and goodwill, provide technical knowledge to less developed countries, broaden the perspectives of American students who interact with foreign students on campus, and increase institutional enrollments. These students represent the "intellectual and social elite of their countries and frequently return to positions of authority and influence, either nationally or internationally" (Hull, 1978, p. 3). For this reason, the U.S. government has

K R. Pyle (ed.). *Guiding the Development of Foreign Students.*
New Directions for Student Services, no. 36. San Francisco: Jossey-Bass, Winter 1986.

encouraged enrollment of foreign students in the nation's institutions of higher education.

The recent increase in the number of foreign students in the United States has been accompanied by a number of research projects that have been conducted since the early 1950s. Many of these studies have focused on either the admission and academic performance of foreign students, comparisons of various nationality groups of foreign students and interactions between American and foreign students, the psychological and social impact of the U.S. experience on foreign students, the relationship of academic achievement to attitudes and adjustment, or of foreign students' experience on their return home.

Research Findings

Admission and Academic Performance. Studies related to admission and academic performance of foreign students were conducted by Allen (1965), the American Association of Collegiate Registrars and Admissions Officers (n.d.), Burgess and Marks (1968), Burke (1968), Center (1967), Chongolnee (1978), Coombs (1961), Ellankany (1970), Elting (1970), Farrar (1968), Ford (1969), Halasz (1969), Heil and Aleamoni (1974), Hj:zainuddin (1974), Hountras (1956), Kaplan (1970), Martin (1971), McKnight and Bennett (1956), Melendez-Craig (1970), Moore (1970), Moravcsik (1972), Ohuche (1967), Paraskevopoulos and Dremuk (1968), Pavri (1963), Sanders and Ward (1970), Sharon (1971), Slocum (1984), Stone (1969), Sugimoto (1966), Telleen (1970), Uehara (1969), Van de Guchte (1969), Vroman, Wilcox, and Tscehan (1970, 1971).

According to Spaulding and Flack (1976), a major concern of many of these studies "has been to develop methods of selecting those foreign applicants who are most likely to succeed in American academic institutions. The studies find rather consistently that scores on English language tests such as TOEFL are good predictors of academic success. Other aptitude and achievement tests, SAT, SCAT, GRE, for example, were less useful. Investigation of the applicant's academic record in the home country proved useful in some cases but not in others. The universal value of careful credential evaluation is therefore open to question" (p. 74).

Grade point averages for foreign students were generally found to be about the same as for American students. However, several studies questioned whether grade point average and other measures of academic achievement normally used for American students are appropriate for determining success for foreign students. The research in this area implies that American institutions of higher education generally do not adapt their educational environments to meet the unique academic needs of students from abroad. Also, very little research has been conducted to determine the academic needs of foreign students as related to their career goals after returning home or on how well American higher education meets these needs.

Comparisons of Nationality Groups and Interactions between American and Foreign Students. Comparisons of various nationality groups of foreign students and issues related to interactions between foreign and American students were studied by Bardis (1956), Becker (1966-1967), Goldsen, Suchman, and Williams (1956), Haller and Bray (1959), Hamilton (1979), Klinger (1962), Klinger and Veroff (1964), Marion and Stafford (1980), Nelson (1966-1967), Penn and Durham (1978), Selltiz, Hopson, and Cook (1956), Shaffer and Dowling (1968), and Singh, Huang, and Thompson (1969).

The results of these studies indicate that small colleges in small towns offer the best potential for interaction between American and foreign students, while large universities in large cities offer the least. Other factors related to interaction were the nationality, personality, living arrangement, and extracurricular interests of foreign students. The type of American student most likely to develop meaningful social relationships with foreign students were those who were already interested in international affairs, lived in close proximity to the foreign students, and were friendly, outgoing students in the mainstream of campus social life.

The research found that foreign students tended to view Americans as hardworking, friendly, informal, immature, superficial in friendships, poorly informed about foreign countries, and, on occasion, "superior" in demeanor and unaware of the impact of the United States on other countries. Foreign students generally liked Americans as individuals.

Comparisons of nationality groups of foreign students revealed that those from Latin America and Europe tend to be more satisfied with their experiences in the United States. Spaulding and Flack (1976) note, however, that "similarities between groups of foreign students tend to outweigh the differences and, in some studies, foreign students display more similarities to their American counterparts than differences, suggesting that many problems arise because they are students rather than because they are foreign" (p. 74).

Psychological and Social Impact. The majority of the research projects on foreign students in the United States have focused on the psychological and social impact of the sojourn on the student. Studies investigating the needs, goals, adjustment, attitudes and values, problems, and satisfaction of foreign students have been conducted by Allen and Arafat (1971), Altscher (1976), Antler (1970), Arjona (1956), Arkoff, Thauer, and Elkind (1966), Bae (n.d.), Bailyn and Kelman (1962), Basu (1966), Beals and Humphrey (1957), Becker (1968, 1971, 1973), Bouenazos and Leamy (1974), Breuder (1972), Brickman (1967), Cannon (1959), Center (1967), Chang (1972), Chu and others (1971), Clements (1967), Coelho (1958, 1972), Coelho-Oudegeest (1971), Cohen (1971), Colacicco (1970), Collins (1976), Culha (1974), Davis (1960), Day (1968), Donahue (1970), DuBois (1954, 1956), Dunnett (1977), Forstat (1951), Gabriel (1973), Galtung (1965), Gandhi (1970,

1972), Gezi (1959), Goodwin and Nacht (1984), Guglielmo (1967), Han (1975), Hansen (1982), Heath (1970), Hegazy (1968), Heise (1971), Holland (1956), Hull (1978), Ibrahim (1968), Jammaz (1972), Jarrahi-Zadeh and Eichman (1970), Johnson (1971), Kang (1971, 1972), Kelman and Bailyn (1962), Kiell (1951), Kimmel (1969), Kincaid (1951), Klein, Alexander, and Tseng (1971), Knudsen (1977), Lambert and Bressler (1956), Lee (1981), Markham (1967), Maslog (1967), Miller (1967), Miller and others (1971), Moftakhar (1976), Moghrabi (1982), Moran, Mestenhauser, and Pederson (1974), Morris (1960), Mowlana and McLaughlin (1969), National Association for Foreign Student Affairs (1973), National Association of College Deans, Registrars, and Admissions Officers–National Association for Foreign Student Affairs (1973), Nenyod (1975), Odenyo (1970), Porter (1962), Pratt (1957), Putman (1965), Restivo (1971), Selltiz, Hopson, and Cook (1956), Selltiz and others (1963), Sewell and Davidsen (1956), Sewell, Morris, and Davidsen (1954), Sharma (1971), Shepard (1970), Singh (1976), Smith (1955, 1956), Snipes (1969), Sofola (1967), Stafford and others (1980), Tanner (1968), Ursua (1969), Useem and Hill (1955), Von Dorpowski (1977), Wakita (1971), Win (1971), and Zajonc (1952).

DuBois (1953) notes that foreign students have formal, private, and unconscious reasons for coming to the United States to study, including curiosity, adventure, desire to learn new skills and acquire technical training, and the possibility of immigration to the United States. Factors related to the adjustment process include English language ability, personality characteristics, previous foreign travel, financial status, academic success, differences between the home country and U.S. culture, American image of the home country, interactions with Americans, race and foreign appearance, living arrangement, age, length of stay, field of study, graduate or undergraduate status, religion, size of college, preconceptions and expectations, socioeconomic background, and whether a job is guaranteed on return home.

Bulthuis in Chapter Two (this volume) discusses typical phases of adjustment. Sewell and Davidsen (1956) describe foreign students as either detached observers, promoters, enthusiastic participants, or settlers, depending on their approach to the adjustment process.

According to Hull (1978), "the experience of being a foreign student in the United States is frequently a difficult and unsettling one, involving periods of isolation and loneliness" (p. 3), and "if entry into a U.S. collegiate institution is a major developmental transition for well-prepared American high school graduates, the transition will be more difficult for young people arriving from distinctly different cultures with different educational systems" (p. 9). Sjogren and Shearer (1973) point out that symptoms of culture shock may include frustration and hostility toward the host culture, excessive concern about personal welfare, and fear of being cheated. Problems associated with difficulties in adjusting to the American experience include social withdrawal, inability to sleep well, sexual problems, sadness and depression, academic problems, loss of personal integrity and self-esteem, difficulties with communicating and making friends, financial concerns, and difficulties learning the cultural maze.

One method foreign students use in coping with adjustment to the United States is to interact primarily with other foreign students from their own country. Conational groups offer advice on coping, serve as temporary surrogates for the home society, and compensate for the student's feeling of social isolation. Although these groups may help in the adjustment process, they may also limit contact with Americans and increase foreign students' isolation from the campus social and political structure.

A number of studies have found that the course of adjustment for foreign students follows a U-shaped curve. Arrival and the early part of the stay are characterized by feelings of elation and optimism. As students become more involved in relationships and encounter frustrations in achieving certain goals, they become confused, depressed, and negative toward the host culture. Students who are able to resolve these difficulties and are in the United States for a sufficient length of time usually learn to work effectively and interact positively with Americans and become more positive about the United States. Although this process of adjustment has been confirmed in a number of studies, it is not universally applicable and may even operate in reverse for some students from less-developed countries.

As is noted in Chapter Two (this volume), Spaulding and Flacks' (1976) research on the impact of the U.S. experience on the attitudes and values of foreign students reveals that those "in the United States for up to two or three years change their basic cultural and religious attitudes very little. They appear to move toward greater openmindedness and toward greater value placed on knowledge, and those from countries with constraints in relationships between women and men increase in desiring greater freedom. Career goals and attitudes toward the home country are, however, fairly resistant to change" (p. 26). Other studies have also indicated that students' sojourns result in a broader, less nationalistic view of the world, increased self-confidence, and more realistic views of the home country and of the United States.

Most foreign students arrive with favorable attitudes toward the United States although students from Europe are most likely to be critical at first. Black Africans tend to have initial apprehensions about racial discrimination and many attempt to differentiate themselves from black Americans. Perceptions of the United States by the end of the stay differ from student to student and seem to depend on each student's preconceptions on arrival; the particular personal, social, and academic experience in the United States; and the perceived value of the experience in relation to career and life goals. Research indicates that other factors related to students' views of the United States are length of stay, age, number of American friends, and students' perceptions of the status accorded by Americans to the home country. Lambert and Bressler (1956) found that if foreign students feel that their home country is accorded low status by Americans, this results in a negative view of the United States. Although the views of foreign students toward the United States during the sojourn do not appear to change in a consistent direction, those who begin their stay with more realistic and less idealistic attitudes about the United States seem to be less likely to be disappointed and therefore more likely to have positive attitudes by the end of the stay.

Relationship of Academic Achievement to Attitude and Adjustment. Studies of the relationship of academic achievement with attitude and adjustment were conducted by Basu (1966), Bohn (1957), Clark (1963), Clarke and Ozawa (1970), Deutsch (1965, 1970), Erickson (1970), Frank (1965), Grady (1969), Hagey (1968), Halberstam and Dasco (1965), Halberstam, Rusk, and Taylor (1970), Hill (1966), Jarrahi-Zadeh and Eichman (1970), Keshav (1969), Kimmel and others (1972), Kwochka (1970), Longest (1969), Lozada (1970), Shepard (1970), and Yankelovich (1971).

These studies indicate that academic achievement of foreign students affects and is affected by their attitudes and adjustment, although a cause-and-effect relationship is not proven. Other work has indicated a relationship between academic success and satisfaction with the U.S. experience and between English language difficulties and academic and social adjustment problems. Also, foreign students from cultural backgrounds that differ significantly from those of the United States often have special kinds of academic problems.

What Happens to Foreign Students on Returning Home? Issues related to what happens to foreign students on their return home after studying in the United States were investigated by the Agency for International Development and reported in six publications in 1966 and 1968 and by Basu (1966), Bennett, Passin, and McKnight (1958), Bohn (1957), Carnovsky (1971), Das (1969), Davis (1971, 1973), Deutsch (1965, 1970), Dow (n.d.), Eide (1970), Galtung (1965), Gama and Pederson (1976), Gardner (1963), Glazer (1974), Goodwin and Nacht (1984), Gullahorn and Gullahorn (1963), Hood and Reardon-Anderson (1979), Johnson (1970), Mackson (1975), Mastroianni (1971), McKnight and Bennett (1956), Myers (1972), Ogunbi (1978), Orr (1971), Passin and Bennett (1954), Preston (1966), Ritterband (1968), Susskind and Schell (1968), and Vorapipatana (1967).

These research projects confirm that the academic training received by foreign students in the United States is generally useful on their return home, although there are wide regional differences, and technical knowledge seems to be applied more easily than abstract research skills. Former students indicate that a longer stay in the United States and more practical experiences included in their academic programs would have made their U.S. experience more valuable.

Gullahorn and Gullahorn (1963) found that returned students undergo a reacculturation process in the home country similar to that experienced during the stay abroad. Other research indicates that female foreign students have an especially difficult time readjusting if their home cultures do not allow women the same extent of freedom as allowed in the United States.

Summary

Research on foreign students in the United States indicates that their academic achievement is similar to that of American students and that there is a positive correlation between English language ability and academic success. Interaction between foreign and American students depends on a variety of factors, and foreign students tend to like Americans as individuals while being critical of certain traits.

The adjustment of foreign students to the United States is affected by a variety of factors and differs from student to student. However, certain phases of adjustment, coping strategies, and changes seem to be common among many students who study abroad. Likewise, attitudes of foreign students toward the United States are affected by certain factors, and certain patterns emerge based on these influences.

Research also indicates that academic achievement of foreign students affects and is affected by their attitudes and adjustment. Finally, academic training received in the United States is generally perceived to be useful to students on return home, and returned students undergo a readjustment process in the home country similar to that experienced during the stay.

Future Research Directions

Jacobsen (1963) considers sojourn research as developmental research, similar to studies of childhood and aging that can yield evidence about regularities in adjustment sequences and predictable correlates of phases of adjustment. Research on foreign students studying in the United States has included a variety of methodologies ranging from interviews, to examination of scholastic records, to the use of surveys and tests. Some studies have focused on specific nationality groups on one campus or on several campuses, while others have concentrated on students from a variety of countries on one campus. Smith (1956) found that much of the early research concentrated on individual foreign students during their stay in the United States and paid little attention to the impact of foreign students on American institutions, communities, or students.

Spaulding and Flack (1976) observe that, "although a number of sponsored, large-scale survey studies display a strong disciplinary competence in theory and statistical method, most of the other studies reviewed do not, indicating the need for greater sophistication in studies of this type" (p. 76). Other shortcomings of research in this area are that little effort has been made to replicate previous studies, and very few longitudinal studies have been conducted.

In terms of future research, Cormack (1962) suggests that research should be carried out by a team of professionals from several of the behaviorial sciences and from both the home and host countries. DuBois (1953) points out the need for investigations into the degree, rate, and duration of the changes experienced by students. Coelho (1962) emphasizes the need for comparative short-term and long-term longitudinal studies to clarify what preparatory functions are served by certain coping behavioral patterns in stimulating the students' psychological development during the sojourn or after return home.

Spaulding and Flack (1976) present possible topics for future research, including methods of developing a university climate favorable to international educational exchange, effect of sponsoring agencies on the international commitment of universities, effect on American students of contact with foreign students, impact of exchange programs on home countries, development of counseling techniques appropriate to the cross-cultural situation, and approaches to the education of students whose personalities and upbringing restrict their openness and sensitivity to a foreign culture. They also recommend studies of the relationship of foreign student attitudes and habits to university policies, relationship between black Africans and black Americans, coping behavior of students from different cultures, and longitudinal follow-up studies of students returned home as regards the relevance of their training to needs of their home countries.

Research on foreign students in the United States has produced significant findings that can be useful in improving educational opportunities for students in the future. Because of the importance of this topic, additional research is needed.

References

Agency for International Development, Participant Training Program. *An Evaluation Study: The Indian Participant Training Program,* 1951-1960. New Delhi: USAID, American Embassy, 1966.
Agency for International Development, Participant Training Program. *Far East: An Evaluation Study.* Washington, D.C.: Agency for International Development, 1966.
Agency for International Development, Participant Training Program. *Latin America: An Evaluation Study.* Washington, D.C.: Agency for International Development, 1966.

Agency for International Development, Participant Training Program. *Near East and South Asia: An Evaluation Study.* Washington, D.C.: Agency for International Development, 1966.

Agency for International Development, Participant Training Program. *North Africa: An Evaluation Study.* Washington, D.C.: Agency for International Development, 1966.

Agency for International Development, Participant Training Program. *Ghana–United States: Participant Training Evaluation Survey, 1957-1967.* Accra: Liberty Press, 1968.

Allen, D. E., and Arafat, I. S. "Procreative Family Attitudes of American and Foreign Students." *International Journal of Comparative Sociology,* 1971, *12,* 134-139.

Allen, W. P. *International Student Achievement: English Test Scores Related to First Semester Grades.* Houston, Tx.: University of Houston, 1965.

Altscher, D. C. "A Rationale for a Counseling Program Designed Uniquely for International Students." Paper presented at the annual convention of the American Personnel and Guidance Association, Chicago, April 11-14, 1976.

American Association of Collegiate Registrars and Admissions Officers. *Report of AACRAO-AID Conference "University-Government Cooperation in Programs for Students from Abroad: An Assessment Based on an AACRAO-AID Study."* Washington, D.C.: American Association of Collegiate Registrars and Admissions Officers, n.d.

Antler, L. "Correlates of Home and Host Country Acquaintanceship Among Foreign Medical Residents in the United States." *The Journal of Social Psychology,* 1970, *80,* 49-57.

Arjona, A. Q. "An Experimental Study of the Adjustment Problems of a Group of Foreign Graduate Students and a Group of American Graduate Students at Indiana University." *Dissertation Abstracts,* 1956, *16* (10), 1838.

Arkoff, A., Thauer, F., and Elkind, L. "Mental Health and Counseling Ideas of Asian and American Students." *Journal of Counseling Psychology,* 1966, *13,* 219-223.

Bae, C. K. *The Effect of Traditionalism on Social Adjustment and Brain Drain: A Study of Korean Students at the University of Wisconsin.* Madison: University of Wisconsin, n.d.

Bailyn, L., and Kelman, H. C. "The Effects of a Year's Experience in America on the Self-Image of Scandinavians: A Preliminary Analysis of Reactions to a New Environment." *Journal of Social Issues,* 1962, *18* (1), 30-40.

Bardis, P. D. "Social Distance Among Foreign Students." *Sociology and Social Research,* 1956, *41,* 112-114.

Basu, A. C. "A Study of Graduate Agricultural Students from India at Selected Land-Grant Colleges and Universities in the United States." Unpublished doctoral dissertation, University of Missouri, 1966.

Beals, R. L., and Humphrey, N. D. *No Frontier to Learning: The Mexican Student in the United States.* Minneapolis: University of Minnesota Press, 1957.

Becker, T. "Perceptions and Attitudinal Changes Among Foreign Students on the U.C.L.A. Campus." *Dissertation Abstracts,* 1966-1967, *16,* 3519.

Becker, T. "Patterns of Attitudinal Changes Among Foreign Students." *American Journal of Sociology,* 1968, *73,* 431-442.

Becker, T. "Cultural Patterns and Nationalistic Commitment Among Foreign Students in the United States." *Sociology and Social Research,* 1971, *55,* 467-481.

Becker, T. "Black Africans and Black Americans on an American Campus: The African View." *Sociology and Social Research,* 1973, *57,* 168-181.

74

Bennett, J. W., Passin, H., and McKnight, R. K. *In Search of Identity: The Japanese Overseas Scholar in America and Japan.* Minneapolis: University of Minnesota Press, 1958.

Bohn, R. C. "An Evaluation of the Educational Program for Students from Foreign Countries: Emphasis on Orientation Procedures, Individual Problems, and Psychological Variables." Unpublished doctoral dissertation, Wayne State University, 1957.

Bouenazos, K., and Leamy, M. K. *An Exploratory Study Concerning Attitudes of Foreign Students Enrolled at Western Michigan University.* Kalamazoo: Western Michigan University, 1974.

Breuder, R. L. *A Statewide Study: Identified Problems of International Students Enrolled in Public Community/Junior Colleges in Florida.* Tallahassee: Department of Higher Education, Florida State University, 1972.

Brickman, W. W. *Foreign Students in American Elementary and Secondary Schools.* Philadelphia: Ogontz Plan Committee, International House, 1967.

Burgess, T. C., and Marks, M. M. "English Aural Comprehension Test Scores as a Predictor of Academic Success Among Foreign Students." *Educational and Psychological Measurement,* 1968, *28,* 1229-1230.

Burke, J. D. "The Predictive Validity of English Language Screening Instruments for Foreign Students Entering the University of Southern California." Unpublished doctoral dissertation, University of Southern California, 1968.

Cannon, G. "Foreign Students in the United States." *American Association of University Professors Bulletin,* 1959, *45,* 539-542.

Carey, P., and Mariam, A. "Minoritization: Toward an Exploratory Theory of Foreign Student Adjustment in the United States." *Negro Educational Review,* 1980, *31,* 127-136.

Carnovsky, L. *The Foreign Student in the American Library School. Final Report.* Chicago: Graduate Library School, 1971.

Center, J. "Our Common Challenge in International Education." *Junior College Journal,* 1967, *37,* 14-16.

Chang, H. "A Study of Some Attitudes of Chinese Students in the United States." Unpublished doctoral dissertation, University of Texas at Austin, 1972.

Chongolnee, B. "Academic, Situational, Organismic, and Attitudinal Factors Affecting the Academic Achievement of Foreign Graduate Students at Iowa State University." Unpublished doctoral dissertation, Iowa State University, 1978.

Chu, H., Yeh, E., Klein, M. H., Alexander, A. A., and Miller, M. H. "A Study of Chinese Students' Adjustment in the U.S.A." *Acta Psychologica Taiwanica,* 1971, *13,* 206-218.

Clark, V.E.W. "Ghanaian Students in the United States." Unpublished doctoral dissertation, University of Michigan, 1963.

Clarke, H., and Ozawa, M. *The Foreign Student in the United States.* Madison: School of Social Work, University of Wisconsin, 1970.

Clements, F. *Leadership Training and Summer Enrichment Program: The Lisle Foundation.* Washington, D.C.: Agency for International Development, 1967.

Coelho, G. V. *Changing Images of America: A Study of Indian Students' Perceptions.* Glencoe, Ill.: Free Press, 1958.

Coelho, G. V. "Personal Growth and Educational Development Through Working and Studying Abroad." *Journal of Social Issues,* 1962, *18* (1), 55-67.

Coelho, V. A. "Students from India in the United States: An Exploratory Study of Some Cultural and Religious Attitudes." Unpublished doctoral dissertation, Loyola University of Chicago, 1972.

Coelho-Oudegeest, M. "Cross-Cultural Counseling: A Study of Some Variables in the Counseling of Foreign Students." Unpublished doctoral dissertation, University of Wisconsin, 1971.

Cohen, R. D. "The Functions of a Conational Group of Foreign Students in New York City." Unpublished doctoral dissertation, 1971.

Colacicco, M. G. "A Comparison of Item Responses on the MMPI by Selected American and Foreign Students." Unpublished doctoral dissertation, Purdue University, 1970.

Collins, P. L. "Self-Perceived Problems of International Students Attending Howard University." Unpublished doctoral dissertation, Howard University, Washington, D.C., 1976.

Coombs, P. H. "International Educational Exchange: A Work for Many Hands." *Higher Education*, 1961, *18*, 3-6.

Cormack, M. L. *An Evaluation of Research on Educational Exchange.* Washington, D.C.: Bureau of Educational and Cultural Affairs, U.S. Department of State, 1962.

Cormack, M. L. "International Development Through Educational Exchange." *Review of Educational Research*, 1968, *38*, 293-302.

Culha, M. U. "Needs and Satisfactions of Foreign Students at the University of Minnesota." Unpublished doctoral dissertation, University of Minnesota, 1974.

Das, M. S. "Effects of Foreign Students' Attitudes Toward Returning to the Country of Origin and the National Loss of Professional Skill." Unpublished doctoral dissertation, Oklahoma State University, 1969.

Davis, F. J. "Cultural Perspectives of Middle Eastern Students in America." *The Middle East Journal*, 1960, *14*, 250-264.

Davis, F. J. "The Two-Way Mirror and the U-Curve: America as Seen by Turkish Students Returned Home." *Sociology and Social Research*, 1971, *56*, 29-43.

Davis, F. J. "Problems of Development in Turkey as Seen by Turks Returned Home from Study in American Universities." *Sociology and Social Research*, 1973, *57*, 429-442.

Day, J. R. "A Study of the Differential Effects of Length of Time in the United States on Foreign Graduate and Undergraduate Students with Regard to the Number, Severity, and Category of Groupings of Problems They Experience." Unpublished doctoral dissertation, Oklahoma State University, 1968.

Deutsch, S. E. *International Aspects of Higher Education and Exchange: A Community Study.* Cleveland, Ohio: Case Western Reserve University, 1965.

Deutsch, S. E. *International Education and Exchange: A Sociological Analysis.* Cleveland, Ohio: Case Western Reserve University Press, 1970.

Donahue, F. "The International Student: His Six Roles." *The Clearing House*, 1970, *45* (1), 51.

Dow, T. I. *The Impact of Chinese Students Returned from America with Emphasis on the Chinese Revolution, 1911-1949.* Boca Raton: Florida Atlantic University, n.d.

DuBois, C. "Research in Cross-Cultural Education." *I.I.E. News Bulletin*, 1953, *28*, 5-8.

DuBois, C. "Motivations of Students Coming to the United States." *I.I.E. News Bulletin*, 1954, *29*, 2-7.

DuBois, C. *Foreign Students and Higher Education in the United States.* Washington, D.C.: American Council on Education, 1956.

Dunnett, S. C. *A Study of the Effects of an English Language Training and Orientation Program on Foreign Student Adaptation at the State University of New York at Buffalo.* Buffalo, N.Y.: Council on International Studies, State University of New York at Buffalo, 1977.

76

Eide, I. (ed.). *Students as Links Between Cultures*. Oslo, Norway: Universitetfor-laget, 1970.

Ellakany, F.A.A. "Prediction of Freshman Year Academic Performance of Foreign Students from Preadmission Data." Unpublished doctoral dissertation, New York University, 1970.

Elting, R. A. "The Prediction of Freshman Year Academic Performance of Foreign Students from Preadmission Data." Unpublished doctoral dissertation, New York University, 1970.

Erickson, D. E. "Differential Personality, Academic, and Biographical Characteristics of International Graduate Students at the University of North Dakota." Unpublished doctoral dissertation, University of North Dakota, 1970.

Farrar, R. D. "The Non-Visa Foreign Student at Los Angeles City College: A Study of the Relation of Various Administrative and Academic Factors to the Immigrant Student." Unpublished doctoral dissertation, University of California at Los Angeles, 1968.

Ford, C. C. "A Case Study of the Adaptational Patterns of Asian Graduate Students in Education at Michigan State University." Unpublished doctoral dissertation, Michigan State University, 1969.

Forstat, R. "Adjustment Problems of International Students." *Sociology and Social Research*, 1951, *36*, 25–30.

Frank, W. W. "An Exploratory Study of Attitudes and Perceptions Toward Change Among AID Technical Assistance Program Participants." Unpublished doctoral dissertation, Michigan State University, 1965.

Gabriel, L. R. "Characteristics of Foreign Students on an American Campus." *Journal of the National Association of Women Deans and Counselors*, 1973, *36*, 184.

Galtung, I. E. "The Impact of Study Abroad: A Three-by-Three Nation Study of Cross-Cultural Contact." *Journal of Peace Research*, 1965, *3*, 258–275.

Gama, E.M.P., and Pederson, P. "Readjustment Problems of Brazilian Returnees from Graduate Studies in the United States." *International Journal of Intercultural Relations*, 1976, *4*, 46–59.

Gandhi, R. S. "Conflict and Cohesion in an Indian Student Community." *Human Organization*, 1970, *29*, 95–102.

Gandhi, R. S. "Some Contrasts in the Foreign Student Life-Style." *International Journal of Contemporary Sociology*, 1972, *9*, 34–43.

Gardner, J. A. *A Beacon of Hope: The Exchange-of-Persons Program*. Washington, D.C.: U.S. Government Printing Office, 1963.

Gezi, K. I. *The Acculturation of Middle Eastern Arab Students in Selected American Colleges and Universities*. Washington, D.C.: American Friends of the Middle East, 1959.

Glazer, A. W. "The Migration and Return of Professionals." *International Migration Review*, 1974, *8*, 224–244.

Goldsen, R. K., Suchman, E. A., and Williams, R. M., Jr. "Factors Associated with the Development of Cross-Cultural Social Interaction." *Journal of Social Issues*, 1956, *12* (1), 26–32.

Goodwin, C. D., and Nacht, M. *Fondness and Frustration: The Impact of American Higher Education on Foreign Students with Special Reference to the Case of Brazil*. New York: Ford Foundation, 1984.

Grady, W. E. "Selected Variables Related to Academic Achievement of American and Canadian Male Freshmen at the University of North Dakota." Unpublished doctoral dissertation, University of North Dakota, 1969.

Guglielmo, H. "Rights and Obligations of Foreign Students in an American University." Unpublished doctoral dissertation, University of Arizona, 1967.

Gullahorn, J. T., and Gullahorn, J. E. "An Extension of the U-Curve Hypothesis." *Journal of Social Issues,* 1963, *19* (3), 33-47.

Hagey, A. R. "Academic and Social Adjustment of Middle Eastern Students Attending Oregon Colleges and Universities." Unpublished doctoral dissertation, University of Oregon, 1968.

Halasz, S. C. "University of California, Los Angeles Study II: Graduate Students from Indonesia, Korea, Pakistan, and Thailand: Fall 1959 through Spring 1967." *College and University,* 1969, *45,* 44-54.

Halberstam, J., and Dasco, M. "Foreign and United States Residents in University Affiliated Teaching Hospitals: An Investigation of United States Graduate Medical Education." Paper presented at a meeting of the Committee on Medical Education at the New York Academy of Medicine, 1965.

Halberstam, J., Rusk, H., and Taylor, E. "Foreign Surgical Residents in University-Affiliated Hospitals." *Annals of Surgery,* 1970, *171,* 485-500.

Haller, A. O., and Bray, B. "Attitudes of American Students Differentially Liked by Latin American Students." *Personnel and Guidance Journal,* 1959, *38,* 217-221.

Halls, W. D. *International Equivalences in Access to Higher Education.* Paris: UNESCO, 1971.

Hamilton, J. T. "A Comparison of Domestic and International Students' Perceptions of the University Environment." *Journal of College Student Personnel,* 1979, *20* (5), 443-445.

Han, P. E. "A Study of Goals and Problems of Foreign Graduate Students from the Far East at the University of Southern California." Unpublished doctoral dissertation, University of Southern California, 1975.

Hansen, E. U. "A Brief Statement of Some Needs of Nontraditional Foreign Students in American Colleges and Universities." *Alternative Higher Education: The Journal of Nontraditional Studies,* 1982, *6* (3), 139-141.

Heath, G. L. "Foreign Student Attitudes at International House, Berkeley." *Exchange,* 1970, *5* (3), 66-70.

Hegazy, M. E. "Cross-Cultural Experience and Social Change: The Case of Foreign Study." Unpublished doctoral dissertation, University of Minnesota, 1968.

Heil, D., and Aleamoni, L. *Assessment of the Proficiency in the Use and Understanding of English by Foreign Students as Measured by the Test of English as a Foreign Language.* Urbana: Office of Instructional Resources, Measurement and Research Division, University of Illinois, 1974.

Heise, J. O. "The Relationship of Foreign Student's Educational and Vocational Values to Background Variables and Perceived Institutional Press." Unpublished doctoral dissertation, Stanford University, 1971.

Hendricks, G. L., and Skinner, K. A. "Adaptive Social Patterns of Foreign Students." *Journal of College Student Personnel,* 1977, *18,* 124-127.

Hill, J. H. "An Analysis of a Group of Indonesian, Thai, Pakistani, and Indian Student Perceptions of Their Problems While Enrolled at Indiana University." Unpublished doctoral dissertation, Indiana University, 1966.

Hj:zainuddin, T. B. "Factors Associated with the Academic Performance of Malaysian Students at Lousiana State University." Unpublished master's thesis, Lousiana State University, 1974.

Holland, K. "Statistics and Comments on Exchange with the United States." *International Social Science Bulletin,* 1956, *8* (4), 628-637.

Hood, M.A.G., and Reardon-Anderson, K. *235,000 Foreign Students in U.S. Colleges and Universities.* Washington, D.C.: Agency for International Development, Office of International Training, 1979.

78

Hountras, P. T. "Academic Probation Among Foreign Graduate Students." *School and Society*, 1956, *84*, 157-176.

Hull, W. F., IV. *Foreign Students in the United States of America: Coping Behavior Within the Educational Environment*. New York: Praeger Publishers, 1978.

Ibrahim, S.E.M. "Political Attitudes of an Emerging Elite: A Case Study of the Arab Students in the United States." Unpublished doctoral dissertation, University of Washington, 1968.

Jacobsen, E. H. "Sojourn Research: A Definition of the Field." *Journal of Social Issues*, 1963, *19* (3), 123-129.

Jammaz, A.I.A. "Saudi Students in the United States: A Study of Their Adjustment Problems." Unpublished doctoral dissertation, Michigan State University, 1972.

Jarrahi-Zadeh, A., and Eichman, W. J. "The Impact of Socio-Cultural Factors on Middle Eastern Students in the United States." *Exchange*, 1970, *5* (3), 82-94.

Johnson, D.C. "Asian Alumni Look Back on Their American Experiences." *Exchange*, 1970, *6* (1), 77-81.

Johnson, D.C. "Problems of Foreign Students." *Exchange*, 1971, *7* (2), 61-68.

Kang, T. S. "Name Change and Acculturation: Chinese Studies on an American Campus." *Pacific Sociological Review*, 1971, *14*, 403-412.

Kang, T. S. "A Foreign Student Group as an Ethnic Community." *International Review of Modern Sociology*, 1972, *2*, 72-82.

Kaplan, R. B. "NAFSA in the Mod Mod World." *Exchange*, 1970, *6* (2), 68-75.

Kelman, H. C., and Bailyn, L. "Effects of Cross-Cultural Experience on National Images: A Study of Scandinavian Students in America." *Journal of Conflict Resolution*, 1962, *6* (9), 319-334.

Keshav, D. S. "Indian Students in the United States." *Exchange*, 1969, *4* (4), 43-59.

Kiell, N. "Attitudes of Foreign Students." *Journal of Higher Education*, 1951, *22*, 188-194.

Kimmel, P. *Orientation of AID Trainees at the Washington International Center.* Washington, D.C.: Office of International Training, Agency for International Development, 1969.

Kimmel, P., Ockey, W. C., and Sander, H. J. *Final Report: International Training Assessment Program.* Washington, D.C.: Development Education and Training Research Institute, The American University, 1972.

Kincaid, H. V. *A Preliminary Study of the Goals and Problems of the Foreign Students in the United States.* Menlo Park, Calif.: Stanford Research Institute, 1951.

Klein, M. H., Alexander, A. A., and Tseng, K. "The Foreign Student Adaptation Program: Social Experiences of Asian Students." *Exchange*, 1971, *6* (3), 77-90.

Klinger, R. B. "Moral Values Across Cultures." *Personnel and Guidance Journal*, 1962, *41* (2), 139-143.

Klinger, R. B., and Veroff, J. "Cross-Cultural Dimensions in Expressed Moral Values." *Personnel and Guidance Journal*, 1964, *42* (9), 899-903.

Knudsen, R. G. "A Fault Tree Approach to an International Education Program: California State University and Colleges." Unpublished doctoral dissertation, California State University, 1977.

Kwochka, V. F. "A Survey of United States Students Regarding the Effects of Their Residence in the International House of New York." Unpublished doctoral dissertation, Columbia University, 1970.

Lambert, R. D., and Bressler, M. *Indian Students on an American Campus.* Minneapolis: University of Minnesota Press, 1956.

Lee, M. *Needs of Foreign Students from Developing Nations at U.S. Colleges and Universities.* Washington, D.C.: National Association for Foreign Student Affairs, 1981.

Longest, J. W. *Evaluating Orientation for Foreign Students.* Ithaca: College of Agriculture at Cornell, State University of New York, 1969.

Lozada, R.C.B. "Foreign Students at Purdue University: A Study of Selected Personal and Academic Characteristics in Relation to Current Experiences and Future Expectations." Unpublished doctoral dissertation, Purdue University, 1970.

McKnight, R. K., and Bennett, J. W. "Liberation or Alienation: The Japanese Woman Student in America." *I.I.E. News Bulletin,* 1956, *31,* 38–47.

Mackson, C. J. "What Do Foreign Graduates Think About Their U.S. Degree Programs?" *Engineering Education,* 1975, *66,* 830–831.

Markham, J. W. *International Images and Mass Communication Behavior.* Iowa City: School of Journalism, University of Iowa, 1967.

Marion, P. B., and Stafford, T. H. "Residence Hall Proximity to Foreign Students as an Influence on Selected Attitudes and Behaviors of American College Students." *Journal of College and University Student Housing,* 1980, *10* (1), 16–19.

Martin, G. M. "A Model for the Cultural and Statistical Analysis of Academic Achievement of Foreign Graduate Students at the University of North Carolina at Chapel Hill." Unpublished doctoral dissertation, University of North Carolina at Chapel Hill, 1971.

Maslog, C. C. "Filipino and Indian Students' Images: of Themselves, of Each Other, and of the United States." Unpublished doctoral dissertation, University of Minnesota, 1967.

Mastroianni, G. A. "A Study of Attitudes Toward the United States Held by Former Participants in a United States Education Exchange Project in Radio and Television." Unpublished doctoral dissertation, Syracuse University, 1971.

Melendez-Craig, M. "A Study of the Academic Achievement and Related Problems Among Latin American Students Enrolled in the Major Utah Universities." Unpublished doctoral dissertation, Brigham Young University, 1970.

Miller, J. C. "African Students and the Racial Attitudes and Practices of Americans." Unpublished doctoral dissertation, University of North Carolina at Chapel Hill, 1967.

Miller, M. H., Yeh, E., Alexander, A. A., Klein, M. H., Tseng, K., Workneh, F., and Chu, H. "The Cross-Cultural Student: Lessons in Human Nature." *Bulletin of the Menninger Clinic,* 1971, *35,* 128–131.

Moftakhar, H. "A Descriptive Study of Some of the Problems of Iranian Students Attending Oklahoma State University." Unpublished doctoral dissertation, 1976.

Moghrabi, K. "Educating Foreigners in the United States." *Improving College and University Teaching,* 1982, *20,* 329–332.

Moore, F. G. "International Education in the Seventies: Revolution or Turmoil on the Campus." *International Educational and Cultural Exchange,* 1970, *6,* 34–47.

Moran, R., Mestenhauser, J., and Pederson, P. "Dress Rehearsal for a Cross-Cultural Experience." *Exchange,* 1974, *10,* 23–25.

Moravcsik, M. J. "The Physics of Interviewing Project." *Exchange,* 1972, *8* (1), 16–22.

Morris, R. *The Two-Way Mirror.* Minneapolis: University of Minnesota Press, 1960.

Mowlana, H., and McLaughlin, G. "Some Variables Interacting with Media Exposure Among Foreign Students." *Sociology and Social Research,* 1969, *53,* 511–522.

Myers, R. G. *Education and Emigration, Study Abroad, and Migration of Human Resources.* New York: David McKay, 1972.

National Association for Foreign Student Affairs. *Report of the NAFSA Task Force on Intercultural Communications Workshops.* Washington, D.C.: National Association for Foreign Student Affairs, 1973.

National Association of College Deans, Registrars, and Admissions Officers–National Association for Foreign Student Affairs. *What's Happening with U.S.–Foreign Student Relations at Predominantly Black Colleges?* Washington, D.C.: National Association for Foreign Student Affairs, 1973.

Nelson, D. "The Impact of Foreign Undergraduate Students on American Undergraduate Education." *Dissertation Abstracts*, 1966–1967, *27*, 2010.

Nenyod, B. "Analysis of Problems Perceived by Foreign Students Enrolled in State Colleges and Universities in the State of Texas." Unpublished doctoral dissertation, East Texas State University, 1975.

Odenyo, A. O. "Africans and Afro-Americans on Campus: A Study of Some of the Relationships Between Two Minority Subcommunities." Unpublished doctoral dissertation, University of Minnesota, 1970.

Ogunbi, A. J. "The Perceived Relevance of Foreign Students' Training to Their Role as Future Change Agents in National Development." Unpublished doctoral dissertation, Michigan State University, 1978.

Ohuche, R. O. "Scholastic Factors Pertaining to the Academic Achievement of Nigerian Students in the United States." Unpublished doctoral dissertation, Iowa State University, 1967.

Orr, J. D., Jr. "The Foreign Scholar Returned Home: A Review of Selected Research." Unpublished doctoral dissertation, Columbia University, 1971.

Paraskevopoulos, J., and Dremuk, R. "Factors Relating to Application Statistics and Enrollment Yield for Foreign Students." Urbana: University of Illinois, 1968.

Passin, H., and Bennett, J. W. "The American-Educated Japanese." *The Annals of the American Academy of Political and Social Science*, 1954, *295*, 83–107.

Pavri, D. M. "A Study of the Scholastic Achievement and Related Problems of Foreign Graduate Students at the University of Virginia from 1957 to 1961." Unpublished doctoral dissertation, University of Virginia, 1963.

Penn, J. R., and Durham, M. L. "Dimensions of Cross-Cultural Interaction." *Journal of College Student Personnel*, 1978, *19* (3), 264–267.

Porter, J. W. "The Development of an Inventory to Determine the Problems of Foreign Students." Unpublished doctoral dissertation, Michigan State University, 1962.

Pratt, D. "The Relation of Culture Goals to the Mental Health of Students Abroad." *International Social Science Bulletin*, 1957, *8* (4), 597–604.

Preston, H. O. *Operations of the Participant Training Program of the Agency for International Development.* Washington, D.C.: Agency for International Development, 1966.

Pruitt, F. J. "The Adaptation of Foreign Students on American Campuses." *Journal of NAWDAC*, 1978, *41*, 144–147.

Putnam, I., Jr. "The Foreign Student Adviser and His Institution in International Student Exchange." In *Handbook for Foreign Student Advisers.* Washington, D.C.: International Student Exchange, National Association for Foreign Student Affairs, 1965.

Restivo, S. P. "Visiting Foreign Scientists at American Universities: A Study of the Third Culture of Science." Unpublished doctoral dissertation, Michigan State University, 1971.

Rising, M. N., and Copp, B. M. *Adjustment Experiences of Nonimmigrant Foreign Students at the University of Rochester, 1967–1968.* Rochester, N.Y.: University of Rochester, 1968.

Ritterband, P. "Out of Zion: The Nonreturning Israeli Students." Unpublished doctoral dissertation, Columbia University, 1968.

Ruscoe, G. *Latin American Students in United States Colleges and Universities.* Washington, D.C.: National Association for Foreign Student Affairs, 1968.

Sanders, I. T., and Ward, J. G. *Bridges to Understanding.* New York: McGraw-Hill, 1970.

Scott, F. D. *The American Experiences of Swedish Students: Retrospect and Aftermath.* Minneapolis: University of Minnesota Press, 1956.

Selby, H., and Woods, C. "Foreign Students at a High-Pressure University." *Sociology of Education,* 1966, *39,* 138-154.

Selltiz, C., Cook, S., Harvel, J., and Christ, J. *Attitudes and Social Relations of Foreign Students.* Minneapolis: University of Minnesota Press, 1963.

Selltiz, C., Hopson, A. L., and Cook, S. W. "The Effects of Situational Factors on Personal Interaction Between Foreign Students and Americans." *Journal of Social Issues,* 1956, *12* (1), 33-44.

Sewell, W. H., and Davidsen, O. M. "The Adjustment of Scandinavian Students." *Journal of Social Issues,* 1956, *12* (1), 9-19.

Sewell, W. H., Morris, R. T., and Davidsen, O. M. "Scandinavian Students' Image of the United States: A Study in Cross-Cultural Education." *Annals of the American Academy of Political and Social Science,* 1954, *295,* 126-145.

Shaffer, R. H., and Dowling, L. R. "Foreign Students and Their American Friends." *School and Society,* 1968, *96,* 245.

Sharma, S. "A Study to Identify and Analyze Adjustment Problems Experienced by Noneuropean Graduate Students Enrolled in Selected Universities in the State of North Carolina." Unpublished doctoral dissertation, University of North Carolina at Greensboro, 1971.

Sharon, A. T. *Test of English as a Foreign Language as a Moderator of Graduate Record Examination Scores in Prediction of Foreign Students' Grades in Graduate School.* Princeton, N.J.: Educational Testing Service, 1971.

Shepard, N. E. "The Acculturation of Foreign Students in Southern Colleges and Universities." Unpublished doctoral dissertation, University of Mississippi, 1970.

Singh, H. P. "A Survey of Socioeconomic Problems and Nonreturn of Selected Foreign Graduate Students at the University of Tennessee." Unpublished doctoral dissertation, University of Tennessee, 1976.

Sjogren, C., and Shearer, B. L. "Is Your Institution Really Ready to Admit Foreign Students? Are You?" *College and University,* 1973, *48,* 601-619.

Slocum, J. "Trends and Prospects in Foreign Student Admissions." *College Board Review,* 1984, *132,* 23-25.

Smith, M. B. "Some Features of Foreign-Student Adjustment." *Journal of Higher Education,* 1955, *26,* 231-241.

Smith, M. B. "Attitudes and Adjustment in Cross-Cultural Contact: Recent Studies of Foreign Students." *Journal of Social Issues,* 1956, *12* (1), 4-8.

Snipes, P. D. "Communication Behavior and Personal Adjustment Among American and Foreign Students at Indiana University." Unpublished doctoral dissertation, Indiana University, 1969.

Sofola, J. A. "American-Processed Nigerians: A Study of the Adjustment and Attitudes of Nigerian Students in the United States of America." Unpublished doctoral dissertation, American University, 1967.

Spaulding, S., and Flack, M. J. *The World's Students in the United States: A Review and Evaluation of Research on Foreign Students.* New York: Praeger, 1976.

Stafford, T. H., Marion, P. B., and Salter, M. L. "Adjustment of International Students." *NASPA Journal,* 1980, *18* (1), 40-45.

Stone, B. "Gaps in Graduate Training of Students from Abroad." *Science,* 1969, 1118.

Sugimoto, R. A. "The Relationship of Selected Predictive Variables to Foreign Student Achievement at the University of California, Los Angeles." Unpublished doctoral dissertation, University of Southern California, 1966.

Susskind, C., and Schell, L. *Exporting Technical Education: A Survey and Case Study of Foreign Professionals with U.S. Graduate Degrees*. New York: Institute of International Education, 1968.

Tanner, S. "An Investigation of Friendship Patterns of Foreign Students." Occasional paper no. 1. Ann Arbor: International Center, University of Michigan, 1968.

Telleen, J.G.J. "A Predictive Model of the Cumulative Academic Achievement of Graduate Students from India." Unpublished doctoral dissertation, University of Michigan, 1970.

Uehara, S. *A Study of Academic Achievement of F-1 Classed Aliens and Other Non-immigrant Temporary Students at Kapiolani Community College*. Honolulu: Kapiolani Community College, 1969.

Ursua, A. R. "The Relationship Between Adeptness in the English Language and Social Adjustment of Foreign Graduate Students." Unpublished doctoral dissertation, Catholic University of America, Washington, D.C., 1969.

Useem, J., and Hill, R. *The Western-Educated Man in India*. New York: Dryden Press, 1955.

Van de Guchte, M. "The Effect of Aural and Visual Cues on the Rating of the Speech of Foreign Students." Unpublished doctoral dissertation, Michigan State University, Ann Arbor, 1969.

Von Dorpowski, H. "The Problems of Oriental, Latin American, and Arab Students in U.S. Colleges and Universities as Perceived by These Foreign Students and Foreign Student Advisers." Unpublished doctoral dissertation, Pennsylvania State University, 1977.

Vorapipatana, K. "A Study of the Thai Graduates' Training Program in the Field of Education from the United States." Unpublished doctoral dissertation, University of Utah, 1967.

Vroman, C., Wilcox, L., and Tschan, R. "Research on AID-Sponsored Students." *College and University*, 1970, *45* (9), 717–723.

Vroman, C., Wilcox, L., and Tschan, R. *The AACRAO-AID Participant Selection and Placement Study*. Washington: D.C.: Agency for International Development, Office of International Training, 1971.

Wakita, K. *Asian Studies Survey—Spring 1970*. Los Angeles: Los Angeles City College, 1971.

Win, U. K. "A Study of the Difficulties Indian and Japanese Students Encountered in Six Problem Areas at the University of Southern California, 1969-1970." Unpublished doctoral dissertation, University of Southern California, 1971.

Yankelovich, D. *A Preliminary Study on Foreign Students in America: The Effects of Today's Campus Environment on Their Attitudes Toward America*. Washington, D.C.: U.S. Department of State, 1971.

Zajonc, R. B. "Aggressive Attitudes of the 'Stranger' as a Function of Conformity Pressures." *Human Relations*, 1952, *5*, 205–216.

Paul B. Marion is director of higher education for the State of Arkansas. He is the immediate past chairperson of ACPA Commission X.

Our ability to affect the future of international student development will depend on our willingness to challenge and handle current issues and trends.

The Future of International Student Development

Barbara A. Clark, K Richard Pyle

We have all heard the saying that the "future is tied to the past." The authors of these chapters have given us an understanding of the past and the current issues and challenges of the present. Edith and Emil Spees challenged us in Chapter One to examine our attitudes toward foreign students and how these can inhibit or promote an environment of growth on our campuses. In Chapter Two Jill Bulthuis helped us understand that there is no such thing as a typical foreign student and that differences in values can limit our communication and understanding. The reality of attitude and value differences have been primary challenges in the past and will no doubt be issues of the future. The antecedents of attitudes and values are deeply rooted in culture. As long as there are different cultures, we will no doubt be faced with issues involving attitudes and values. The richness and variety of culture is something we want to protect. It provides the basis which makes the foreign student unique and for many of us is one of the major motivations for involvement in working with foreign students. Therefore, will the future provide any real differences from the past? Will we be able to cope successfully with the pending increase of foreign students? To answer these questions we must synthesize the information of this book, specify the current issues and challenges, and determine the implications for the future.

K R. Pyle (ed.). *Guiding the Development of Foreign Students.*
New Directions for Student Services, no. 36. San Francisco: Jossey-Bass, Winter 1986.

Current Issues, Challenges, and Recommendations

Theory and Practice. An integrated theory of student development as it relates to foreign students is needed if we are to have any real impact on facilitating foreign student growth. Storey (1982) claims that student development theory represents a conflict in values when applied to foreign students. Student development theory is rooted in the values of the American culture and educational system, and thus the assumptions we make cannot be considered value free. It is important that we develop a theory and approach that cuts across cultures and value systems and that integrates principles considered to be international. The members of the American College Personnel Association (ACPA) and the National Association for Foreign Student Affairs (NAFSA) must cooperate in developing such a theory, which will help provide new meaning to international education as well as a badly needed foundation for solving problems and developing programs and approaches. This would be an excellent and meaningful service that Commission X, "International Dimensions of Student Development," of ACPA could undertake.

Effective Preparation for Professionals. Foreign student advisers and professionals in the international arena must develop standards that clearly differentiate the skills and competencies needed for effective work with foreign students. Mestenhauser (1976) challenges foreign student advisers by saying: "In describing ourselves we often take pride in being jacks of all trades, plus more" (p. 9). Pointing out that foreign student advisers come from many different backgrounds, Mestenhauser claims that they operate as a "semi-profession" and calls for the establishment of a "professional culture" within their professional association, the National Association for Foreign Student Affairs (NAFSA). Although some institutions offer cross-cultural counseling and coursework in intercultural communication as part of their graduate degree programs, many do not. Graduate programs can respond to this issue by offering coursework in cross-cultural counseling, intercultural communications, and seminars in foreign student services. The method for implementing these changes within departments is uncertain. Althen (1983) argues that foreign student advisers often lack power to make changes on their campuses, yet they may have "influence." It is suggested that this influence be used as a means to develop professional standards within such organizations as NAFSA and ACPA and the National Association of Student Personnel Administrators (NASPA) and that this influence also be used as leverage to implement these standards within the colleges and universities.

Professional Integration, Reentry, and Alumni Programs. Presently, little is done to assist foreign students in developing the new roles that their new degrees and return to their home countries bring about. More help is needed with such problems of reentry. Schieffer (1983) identifies and clarifies the issue: "For foreign students, the passage from academic to professional is complicated by having to make an adjustment from a developed to a developing world. Colleges and universities in the United States are not generally equipped to handle professional integration problems and are therefore unable to give meaningful guidance to the student returning to the developing world. Having returned home, the student from the developing world does not find institutions or services to help in this transition process. Nor can the student generally look to parents or peers for guidance of this type. Parents and peers are likely to be confused themselves by the changes and transitional problems of the returned student" (p. 2). There is currently an emphasis on career counseling and career development in student affairs, but little of this attention is directed toward the foreign student population. In addition, as was mentioned in Chapter Five, it is important for us to be aware of how foreign students' academic programs relate to types of work they will be qualified for in their home countries. Staying in touch with students after their return home can be a crucial step in the process of reentry. Alumni programs should include foreign alumni in their programs. Whenever possible, alumni trips abroad should include brief visits with foreign alumni. Other returning students in the student's home country can be of valuable assistance in easing readjustment to the student's home country conditions. Finally, foreign student offices can benefit from alumni who have returned home. They can be of assistance in recruiting future students and providing predeparture orientation programs for prospective students. Foreign alumni programs are relatively new in the United States, and they are often directed by the foreign student office instead of the college or university's alumni center (Goetzl and Stritter, 1980). Regardless of where these programs are directed, foreign alumni can be of value to the goals of human development. Our challenge, therefore, is to expand our concepts toward more far-reaching goals than the traditional four years of college and to examine our current career counseling and advising services.

Family Services. As mentioned in Chapter One, an important concern of foreign graduate students is the amount and quality of services provided to their families who accompany them to the United States or join them at a later date. Like Pat Cross's (1971) "new" students, spouses in this category are struggling with the desire to enhance their education at a pace and time convenient to their lives. In addition, many of their children who attend local schools create conflicts for their families as they become accustomed to the life and culture of the United States. Yet foreign families have other issues that go beyond Cross's conception of nontraditional students in that these families must cope with strict immigration regulations, language problems, and cultural problems that generally cause confusion and disorientation. We must therefore seek ways in which we can promote student development for this isolated group on our campuses.

Foreign Student Services in the Future

Although it is difficult to make long-range predictions about any aspect of student services, there are certain trends that have been identified as relevant now that can provide insight into what we can expect in the future. The following is based on effectively meeting the above challenges and assumes that world conditions will remain relatively stable.

1. *Foreign student advisers and support personnel will be required to meet high-level training standards and a credentialing process.* This credentialing program will require competence in cross-cultural communication skills as well as knowledge and expertise in such areas as visa requirements and immigration procedures. Credentialed staff will be necessary as a part of the requirements for an institution's accreditation. This will enhance the quality of services provided.

2. *Research on foreign student development will increase.* As more faculty become involved in international work, research will increase that will test existing theories of the foreign population. However, the results will necessitate the development of new theories and instruments for measuring these theories, since researchers will find it increasingly difficult to develop statistical instruments to measure variables cross culturally.

3. *Professional association networking will increase.* NAFSA and ACPA Commission X will have a close collaborative relationship that will provide important cross-fertilization. Areas of concentrations will be (1) theory development, (2) international networking, (3) research, and (4) certification standards for individuals working with foreign student populations.

4. *Utilization of international cross-cultural settings to promote student development for U.S. students will increase.* The value of an overseas cross-cultural experience that promotes the growth of U.S. students will be more fully recognized and developed. Students will be placed in settings and service assignments related to their career interests. Foreign students will be used as trainers and resource persons in these programs. Research has already pointed out the value of such programs in enhancing student development (Pyle, 1981). The data suggest that an overseas setting can provide a high quality student development laboratory.

Conclusion

It is said that Francisco Miranda, who attended Yale in 1784, was the first foreign student to study in the United States (Putnam, 1965). Since that time thousands of foreign students have participated in the U.S. educational process. Are we better off? The answer has to be yes! Where else can the potential for world peace and understanding take place other than in the manner in which we care for and assist in the education of students from other lands? Much needs to be done if we are to realize the dreams of the above scenario. However, the possibilities exist and the pieces are in place. What is needed is the commitment to human development to make these dreams a reality.

References

Althen, G. *The Handbook of Foreign Student Advising*. Yarmouth, Maine: Intercultural Press, 1983.

Cross, K. P. *Beyond the Open Door: New Students to Higher Education*. San Francisco: Jossey-Bass, 1971.

Goetzl, S., and Stritter, J. (eds.). "Foreign Alumni: Overseas Links for U.S. Institutions." Washington, D.C.: National Association for Foreign Student Affairs, 1980.

Mestenhauser, J. "Are We Searching for Identity as Professionals, Semiprofessionals, or Dedicated Good Guys?" *NAFSA Newsletter*, 1976, 27 (8), 7, 9-11.

Putnam, I., Jr. "The Foreign Student Adviser and His Institution in International Student Exchange." In *Handbook for Foreign Student Advisers*. Washington, D.C.: International Student Exchange, National Association for Foreign Student Affairs, 1965.

Pyle, K R. "International Service? Learning: Impact on Student Development?" *Journal of College Student Personnel*, November 1981, pp. 509-514.

Schieffer, K. J. "Introduction." In M. A. Hood and K. J. Schieffer (eds.), *Professional Integration: A Guide for Students from the Developing World*. Washington, D.C.: National Association for Foreign Student Affairs, 1983.

Storey, K. E. "The Student Development Professional and the Foreign Student: A Conflict of Values." *Journal of College Student Personnel*, 1982, 23 (1), 66-70.

Barbara A. Clark is a foreign student adviser at the University of Iowa. She is an active member of both NAFSA and ACPA.

K Richard Pyle is a counseling psychologist and coordinator of counseling at the University of Texas, Austin. He is a past chairperson of ACPA Commission X and has been active in international work with the Peace Corps.

Index

A

Abd-Ella, M., 17, 52, 53, 62
Academic performance: and admissions criteria, 66; and attitude and adjustment, 70
Adams, E. A., 36, 37
Adjustment: and academic achievement, 70; social and cultural, 53; stages of, for foreign students, 26
Admission. *See* Recruitment and admissions
Advising: and academic relevance, 53, 55-56; analysis of, 51-63; competence for, 55-56; and educational system, 25-26, 52-53, 55; and financial problems, 32-33, 52; guidelines for, 53-56; and language difficulties, 52, 54-55; needs for, 52-53; and social and cultural adjustment, 53; training and credentialing for, 84, 86
Africa, 6, 23, 24, 33, 57, 58, 69, 72, 73, 74, 79, 80, 81
Agency for International Development (AID), 70, 72, 73, 76, 78, 80, 82
Aleamoni, L., 66, 77
Alexander, A. A., 56, 57, 58, 61, 62, 68, 74, 78, 79
Allen, D. E., 67, 73
Allen, W. P., 66, 73
Althen, G., 48, 49, 53, 57, 61, 84, 87
Altscher, D. C., 67, 73
American Association for Counseling and Development (AACD), 11, 15, 17
American Association for Higher Education (AAHE), 11
American Association for State Colleges and Universities (AASCU), 11
American Association of Community and Junior Colleges (AACJC), 15
American Association of Collegiate Registrars and Admissions Officers (AACRAO), 32, 33, 66, 73, 82
American College Personnel Association (ACPA), 15; Commission X of, 1, 84, 86

American-Midwest Educational and Training Services (AMID-EAST), 34
Antler, L., 67, 73
Arafat, I. S., 67, 73
Arjona, A. Q., 67, 73
Arkoff, A., 67, 73
Asia, 5, 7, 12, 20, 21, 22, 23, 29-30, 36, 40, 57, 58, 72, 73, 74, 75, 76, 77, 78, 79, 80, 81, 82
Association for College Admissions Counselor, 17
Association of College Unions-International (ACU-I), 11, 15, 17
Association of International Education Administrators (AIEA), 15-16

B

Bae, C. K., 67, 73
Bailyn, L., 67, 68, 73, 78
Baker, S. B., 58, 62
Barber, E. G., 20, 21, 22, 27
Bardis, P. D., 67, 73
Barr, M. J., 1n
Basu, A. C., 67, 70, 73
Beals, R. L., 67, 73
Beauvais, F., 61
Becker, T., 67, 73
Bennett, J. W., 66, 70, 74, 79, 80
Binitie, A., 57, 61
Bohn, R. C., 70, 74
Bouenazos, K., 67, 74
Bray, B., 67, 77
Brazil, 76
Brennan, J., 62
Bressler, M., 68, 70, 78
Breuder, R. L., 67, 74
Brickman, W. W., 67, 74
Brohm, J. F., 30, 37
Bulthuis, J. D., 2, 19, 27, 52, 68, 83
Burgess, T. C., 66, 74
Burke, J. D., 66, 74
Burks, L. A., 17, 52, 53, 62
Business community, and international programs, 14

U.S. Postal Service
STATEMENT OF OWNERSHIP, MANAGEMENT AND CIRCULATION
Required by 39 U.S.C. 3685

1A. TITLE OF PUBLICATION		1B. PUBLICATION NO.							2. DATE OF FILING
New Directions for Student Services		4	4	9	0	7	0		9/26/86

3. FREQUENCY OF ISSUE	3A. NO. OF ISSUES PUBLISHED ANNUALLY	3B. ANNUAL SUBSCRIPTION PRICE
Quarterly	4	$30 indv/$40 inst

4. COMPLETE MAILING ADDRESS OF KNOWN OFFICE OF PUBLICATION *(Street, City, County, State and ZIP+4 Code) (Not printers)*

433 California St., San Francisco (SF County), CA 94104

5. COMPLETE MAILING ADDRESS OF THE HEADQUARTERS OF GENERAL BUSINESS OFFICES OF THE PUBLISHER *(Not printer)*

433 California St., San Francisco (SF COunty) CA 94104

6. FULL NAMES AND COMPLETE MAILING ADDRESS OF PUBLISHER, EDITOR, AND MANAGING EDITOR *(This item MUST NOT be blank)*
PUBLISHER *(Name and Complete Mailing Address)*

Jossey-Bass Inc., Publishers, 433 California St., S.F., CA 94104

EDITOR *(Name and Complete Mailing Address)*

Margaret J. Barr, M. Lee Upcraft, Sadler Hall, Texas Christian University, Fort Worth, Texas 76129

MANAGING EDITOR *(Name and Complete Mailing Address)*

Allen Jossey-Bass, Jossey-Bass Publishers, 433 California St., S.F., CA 94104

7. OWNER *(If owned by a corporation, its name and address must be stated and also immediately thereunder the names and addresses of stockholders owning or holding 1 percent or more of total amount of stock. If not owned by a corporation, the names and addresses of the individual owners must be given. If owned by a partnership or other unincorporated firm, its name and address, as well as that of each individual must be given. If the publication is published by a nonprofit organization, its name and address must be stated.) (Item must be completed.)*

FULL NAME	COMPLETE MAILING ADDRESS
Jossey-Bass Inc., Publishers	433 California St., S.F., CA 94104
For Names and addresses of stockholders, see attached list.	

8. KNOWN BONDHOLDERS, MORTGAGEES, AND OTHER SECURITY HOLDERS OWNING OR HOLDING 1 PERCENT OR MORE OF TOTAL AMOUNT OF BONDS, MORTGAGES OR OTHER SECURITIES *(If there are none, so state)*

FULL NAME	COMPLETE MAILING ADDRESS
Same as #7	

9. FOR COMPLETION BY NONPROFIT ORGANIZATIONS AUTHORIZED TO MAIL AT SPECIAL RATES *(Section 423.12 DMM only)*
The purpose, function, and nonprofit status of this organization and the exempt status for Federal income tax purposes *(Check one)*

(1) ☐ HAS NOT CHANGED DURING PRECEDING 12 MONTHS	(2) ☐ HAS CHANGED DURING PRECEDING 12 MONTHS	*(If changed, publisher must submit explanation of change with this statement.)*

10.	EXTENT AND NATURE OF CIRCULATION *(See instructions on reverse side)*	AVERAGE NO. COPIES EACH ISSUE DURING PRECEDING 12 MONTHS	ACTUAL NO. COPIES OF SINGLE ISSUE PUBLISHED NEAREST TO FILING DATE
A.	TOTAL NO. COPIES *(Net Press Run)*	2300	2268
B.	PAID AND/OR REQUESTED CIRCULATION		
1.	Sales through dealers and carriers, street vendors and counter sales	274	185
2.	Mail Subscription *(Paid and/or requested)*	970	860
C.	TOTAL PAID AND/OR REQUESTED CIRCULATION *(Sum of 10B1 and 10B2)*	1244	1045
D.	FREE DISTRIBUTION BY MAIL, CARRIER OR OTHER MEANS SAMPLES, COMPLIMENTARY, AND OTHER FREE COPIES	76	189
E.	TOTAL DISTRIBUTION *(Sum of C and D)*	1320	1234
F.	COPIES NOT DISTRIBUTED		
1.	Office use, left over, unaccounted, spoiled after printing	980	1034
2.	Return from News Agents		
G.	TOTAL *(Sum of E, F1 and 2 - should equal net press run shown in A.)*	2300	2268

11. I certify that the statements made by me above are correct and complete	SIGNATURE AND TITLE OF EDITOR, PUBLISHER, BUSINESS MANAGER, OR OWNER
	[signature] Vice President

PS Form 3526, Dec. 1985   *(See instruction on reverse)*